Streamliner MEMORIES

Mike Schafer

MBI Publishing Company

First published in 1999 by MBI Publishing Company,
729 Prospect Avenue, PO Box 1, Osceola, WI 54020-0001 USA

© Andover Junction Publications, 1999

MBI Publishing Company books are also available at discounts in bulk quantity for industrial or sales-promotional use. For details write to Special Sales Manager at Motorbooks International Wholesalers & Distributors, 729 Prospect Avenue, Osceola, WI 54020-0001 USA.

Library of Congress Cataloging-in-Publication Data
Schafer, Mike.
    Streamliner memories / Mike Schafer.
       p. cm.
      ISBN 0-7603-0619-2 (pbk. : alk. paper)
      1. Express trains—United States. 2. Railroads—United States—
Passenger-cars. I. Title.
TF573.S326   1999
385'.0973—dc21   98-53105

On the front cover: On the eve of Amtrak, April 30, 1971: Streamliners at Chicago Union Station load up for the last time as the era of privately operated passenger trains draws to a close. At right stands Burlington Northern's *California Zephyr* Service train—a remnant of the once-proud *California Zephyr* domeliner—and at far left can be seen the Vista-Dome *North Coast Limited* about to embark on its cross-country journey to the Pacific Northwest. A silvery Burlington diesel powers a lowly commuter train sandwiched by the two great trains of yore. *Jim Heuer*

On the frontispiece: A parlor-lounge car from Rock Island's once-extensive fleet of *Rocket* streamliners reflects an era of posh surroundings and elegant service that were once commonplace on U.S. passenger trains. *Jim Heuer*

On the title page: On the evening of April 24, 1971, Santa Fe's *San Francisco Chief* strikes out of Kansas City, Missouri, for its namesake city still some 2,090 miles distant. Aboard the Chicago-Richmond (California) train, travelers will enjoy a restful ride aboard sleepers and Hi-Level chair cars, with social visits to the Big Dome Lounge and dining car. *Jim Heuer*

On the back cover: Santa Fe Railway's *Texas Chief* basks in late afternoon sun at Chicago's Dearborn Station on July 3, 1970, shortly before its departure for the Lone Star State. By this time tomorrow, the streamliner will have called at Kansas City, Topeka, Oklahoma City, and Fort Worth with a late evening arrival at Houston, its final destination. The *Texas Chief* was just one of several Santa Fe streamliners that provided comfortable, memorable travel for Americans for more than 30 years. *Jim Heuer*

Designed by Rebecca Allen

Printed in China

CONTENTS

ACKNOWLEDGMENTS

Streamliner Memories was a pleasure to do for many reasons, not the least of which was the opportunity to work with other folks who love passenger trains. First, thanks must go to Joe Welsh, my co-author for *Classic American Streamliners*, for which this book, *Streamliner Memories*, in part serves as a companion. Joe is a great sounding board for ideas as well as an excellent source of information about streamliners.

As well, I shine the spotlight on Bob Johnston of Chicago. Bob is one of the few people I know who, even back in the 1960s, had the foresight to photograph things other than the outside of a passenger train. Bob's photos of passenger-train crews at work and passenger-train interiors alive with passengers are a veritable treasure chest of memories. For similar reasons, I'd like to thank longtime friend Jim Heuer for access to his remarkable collection of unique passenger-train images of the late 1960s and early 1970s—on large-format film, no less, for an extra touch of quality.

More accolades, this time to Dave Oroszi, Alvin Schultze, Mike McBride, Jim and Beulah Bauman, Richard Kunz, Ed DeRouin, Joe McMillan, Sandy Goodrick, David W. Salter, and Joe and Janine Petric for their help in this book project. And finally, I thank Steve Esposito and Joyce Mooney, my partners and friends within our own company, Andover Junction Publications, the producer of this book, and the folks at MBI Publishing for making this book possible.

INTRODUCTION

*T*here was a time when streamliners could be found in all four corners of America, from Van Buren, Maine, to San Diego, California, and from Seattle, Washington, to Miami, Florida. Their names were evocative, perfunctory, and sometimes even whimsical: the *Aroostook Flyer*, the *San Diegan*, the *Western Star*, and the *City of Miami*. They provided the public with ground transport at its finest and most comfortable.

The classic American streamliner can be compared to a nova, a star that suddenly becomes many times brighter and then fades. The streamliner era in the United States officially began in 1934 with the roll-out of Union Pacific's M-10000 and Chicago, Burlington & Quincy's *Zephyr* 9900. The two little lightweight, new-from-the-ground-up speedsters were beacons of hope in the Great Depression, proving to railroads across the land that new, comfortable, innovative, high-speed streamlined trains could lure passengers back to the rails.

An explosion of new streamliners soon followed the M-10000 and 9900, tempered only by the World War II years (1941–1945). Shortly after the war the streamliner movement reached unparalleled intensity, only to peak by about the mid-1950s. Although new streamliners continued to be added until the late 1950s, a disturbing decline in passenger revenues had set in. That, and escalating costs, applied the brakes to a short but colorful epoch for the American passenger train.

America's shift in transportation policies and commitments after the war ended the relative monopoly that railroads had held on freight and passenger transportation up to that time. Central to this change was the automobile, the passenger train's principal nemesis since the 1920s. It was joined by a new competitor in the late 1950s, the commercial jetliner.

As both the interstate highway system and jet airliner network grew, America's passenger-train network

In the heyday of the streamliner era after World War II, even the far corners of the country enjoyed streamliner service. In Maine, for example, Bangor & Aroostook Railroad's *Aroostook Flyer* once served the residents of Millinocket, Caribou, Van Buren, and other remote Maine communities. The *Flyer* was streamlined in 1949, an event publicized in this brochure for both the *Flyer* and its companion train, the *Potatoland Special*, which received some new streamlined cars as well. *Mike Schafer collection*

correspondingly shrunk. The conservative and over-regulated railroad industry simply was no match for government-supported "freeways" and air-transport facilities.

A double-whammy in the late 1960s sealed the fate of the privately operated passenger train. First was the U.S. Post Office's shift of mail from rail to trucks and planes, in particular mail sorted aboard Railway Post Office (RPO) cars, an important revenue-producer on many passenger trains. Second was the Pullman Company's closure of its sleeping-car network at the end of 1968. Faced with the added costs of operating their own sleeping cars, many railroads chose simply to eliminate sleeping-car service, turning some overnight streamliners into coach-only operations. The final unraveling was under way.

Had it not been for congressional concern for the future of the passenger train, we might well be the only major country today without intercity passenger trains. But in 1970, President Richard Nixon signed a bill that created the National Railroad Passenger Corporation (Amtrak) to relieve most railroads of the passenger-train burden. Often mistakenly called a government agency, Amtrak is actually a railroad company, but with a controversial twist: The government underwrites its losses.

Travelers to the far southeast end of the United States—Florida—had numerous streamliners at their disposal, including a local Jacksonville-Miami run over the Florida East Coast Railway known as the *Henry M. Flagler.* This postcard shows the train's appearance at the time of its 1939 inaugural. Shortly after, it was extended all the way to Chicago as the *Dixie Flagler.* The real Henry M. Flagler almost single-handedly transformed the state of Florida from wilderness to tourist haven early in the 20th century. *Joe Welsh collection*

Amtrak began operations on May 1, 1971, but —woefully undercapitalized—could continue running only about half of the passenger trains that had been running immediately prior to its startup. Some 150 trains were axed, including many famous liners, from the *City of Los Angeles* to the *Wabash Cannonball.* Streamliners per se didn't really vanish when Amtrak emerged, but it was a whole new order, destined for homogenization under a single new image.

In the aftermath of this extraordinary turning point for the American passenger train lay memories of streamliners of yore—memories in the mind as well as those in the form of timetables, brochures, tickets, dining car china, menus, and photographs. Come aboard *Streamliner Memories* and savor some of these recollections.

Streamliners everywhere: Chicago & North Western's 40th Street Yard facility near downtown Chicago in the late 1940s is full of streamliners and streamliner locomotives being serviced during their layover—streamliners that have arrived from distant points as well as those that will be dispatched west to California, northwest to Oregon, and north to Upper Michigan and Wisconsin later in the day. *Chicago & North Western*

Chapter 1

TWO SPECIAL STREAMLINERS REMEMBERED

*A*s the final warm days of summer 1997 drifted by, anticipation mounted for the impending release of a new book that friend Joe Welsh and I had written, *Classic American Streamliners* (MBI Publishing). A poignantly related (but entirely coincidental) event was also approaching at a railcar shop in Milwaukee, Wisconsin: the completion of a major restoration of Chicago, Burlington & Quincy *Zephyr* 9900.

Zephyr 9900—also known as the *Pioneer Zephyr*—was one of the first two lightweight streamlined passenger trains to grace U.S. rails. The 1934 launchings of Union Pacific's M-10000 streamliner

Re-creating a scene played out 63 years earlier at the Edward G. Budd Manufacturing Company near Philadelphia, Pennsylvania, the craftspeople of Northern Rail Car in Milwaukee tug the restored *Pioneer Zephyr* out before the eyes of the media on September 8, 1997. The *Pioneer Zephyr*—aka *Zephyr* 9900, America's first diesel-powered, lightweight, high-speed streamliner—had just been completely restored for its prominent, new display site at Chicago's Museum of Science and Industry.

Both the M-10000 and *Zephyr* 9900 created quite a stir with the public's imagination, so it was no surprise that toy-train manufacturers began offering replicas of them right away. Models of the M-10000 seem to be more prolific—which is fortunate in the sense that the real train was scrapped during World War II—and they can be found in several scales. The top model is an O-27 gauge 1934 wind-up version by Marx, at one time the world's largest toy manufacturer. The standard-gauge model (in the middle) was issued by Lionel, also in 1934. The bottom model, roughly in HO scale, was also by Marx but made in England in the 1950s for the British market. *Dan Roth collection, Gerry Souter photo for Andover Junction Publications*

and Burlington's *Zephyr* 9900 revolutionized the way railroads and passengers thought about passenger trains.

Both trains were wildly successful, launching the streamliner revolution on a number of U.S. railroads as well as Burlington and Union Pacific. Unfortunately, the M-10000 was scrapped during World War II as part of Union Pacific's contribution to the war effort. *Zephyr* 9900 soldiered (or, more to the point, sprinted) on, operating in various Chicago, Burlington & Quincy assignments until 1960, when the still-gleaming train was

Zephyr 9900's dawn-to-dusk run in May 1934 earned it the reputation of being the world's fastest train, but the streamliner also garnered fame by starring in the movie *Silver Streak*, filmed shortly after the 9900 was outshopped. In the flick, 9900 (its "Burlington Route" nose emblem having been replaced by the name "Silver Streak") whisks an iron lung (then also a new technology) cross country to save a child's life. The 9900 is shown on public display at an unidentified location, probably during its 1934 barnstorm tour of the United States before entering regular service in November of that year. *Ed DeRouin collection*

retired and donated to Chicago's Museum of Science and Industry.

Despite the *Zephyr* 9900's importance to rail transportation, it was relegated to an out-of-the-way location on the museum grounds and only intermittently opened to the public. There 9900 basked in relative obscurity until the mid-1990s when museum folks came up with a better idea: restore and fully display the train.

Project sponsor Grainger Corporation had Northern Rail Car in North Milwaukee, Wisconsin, handle the restoration. Over the course of three years, some 16,000 hours went into returning the little train

The shovel nose of 9900 suggests what it might have been like to look face-to-face with an ancient Roman gladiator. Indeed, Burlington's *Zephyr* fleet theming was largely based on the mystique of Roman mythology. Zephyrus was the Roman god of the West wind.

to its original appearance—and splendor. Meanwhile, the Museum of Science and Industry built a new, high-profile display area for the *Zephyr* in the grand hall linking the museum with its new (spring 1998) underground parking area.

Although my streamliner memories date from the early 1950s, my association with the *Zephyr* 9900 bloomed late. I grew up in an on-line Burlington city—Rockford, Illinois—but quite distant from the 9900's regular haunts—western Illinois, Missouri, Iowa, Nebraska, and Colorado. Consequently, I became cognizant of the train only after it was retired. Beginning in the mid-1960s, the 9900 became an acquaintance only through brief glimpses of it as I sped past the museum on Lake Shore Drive during auto trips to Chicago.

Not until Joe Welsh and I began researching for *Classic American Streamliners* in 1996 did I fully begin to appreciate the importance of Union Pacific's M-10000 and the *Zephyr* 9900. Thus, when the opportunity arose to closely inspect the renovated 9900 upon its rededication at Northern Rail Car on September 8, 1997, I cleared the calendar and headed for Milwaukee.

I joined folks from various media, railroads, and the Museum of Science and Industry for a simple but memorable ceremony. NRC launched it with panache by re-creating the *Zephyr* 9900's original 1934 roll-out from the Budd Company: Workers pulled the train out of the shop with a rope. (Apparently this was done originally to underscore the lightweight nature of the train.) NRC shop forces—about 15 strong—strained against the rope that led into the darkness beyond the open shop door. Slowly, a silver, furrow-browed prow materialized. Then, with most of the power car out of the portal, the workers released the rope and the 9900 shuddered to a halt.

Goose bumps!

Here it was, right before my eyes. One of the two trains that had inspired a whole legion of streamliners that for decades would tie us together as a nation, trains like the *20th Century Limited*, *Super*

Zephyr 9900's interior was restored as closely to its original appearance as feasible. The baggage-coach features leather seats facing the buffet area, behind the glass bulkhead. The baggage section is beyond the buffet area, and the coach seating in this car was the designated smoking area. Not only was the observation lounge chic by 1934 standards, but could work in the "retro-design" era of the 1990s too.

Chief, Broadway Limited, Coast Daylight, Empire Builder, Silver Meteor, City of Los Angeles, and ever so many more. Initially, the crowd stood in quiet awe, about the only audible sound being hundreds of camera shutter clicks. Shortly, the train was rolled back inside, and everyone was invited inside for further inspection.

Resisting all impulse to shove aside elderly ladies and children like George Costanza did in *Seinfeld* episode No. 80, "The Fire," I eagerly, and at last, set foot aboard the stainless-steel celebrity. I headed first to the observation lounge where I took a seat among other media types and passenger-train enthusiasts, among them Robert Bullerman who as a youth had watched the 9900 speed into Chicago on its landmark dawn-to-dusk nonstop Denver-Chicago run on May 26, 1934, and James A. Neubauer, who rode the train's final run on March 20, 1960.

The train interior revealed remarkable restoration work, right down to the John Harbeson–designed lounge chairs, the RPO letter compartments, wall coverings, coach seats, restroom facilities, and tile floors. In due time, we guests dispersed, leaving Northern Rail Car folks the task of preparing the train for its truck trip home to Chicagoland.

This little story doesn't quite end there. Less than two months after my first true rendezvous with the 9900 at Northern Rail Car, I moved back to my home state, to a house I had built next to the former Chicago, Burlington & Quincy *Twin Cities Zephyr* main line through northern Illinois. Aware of my interest in railroading, my retired neighbor, George Ewing, shared some of his reminiscences during one of our neighborly fence talks.

"Mike, I have to tell you about the time in the spring of '34—I was just a lad—when I climbed up

The 9900's coach-observation car gleams under the shop lights of Northern Rail Car as guests inside sample the memories of a time when rail travel was high art. The train can be viewed today, inside and out, at Chicago's Museum of Science and Industry.

on the roof of the grain elevator next to the Burlington tracks in Malden [Illinois] to watch a special train."

Spring of 1934? Special train? I suddenly realized he was talking about the *Zephyr* 9900's famous nonstop Denver-Chicago run!

"That little bugger of a train, Mike, why, she flashed through town like *that* [George swoops his right arm]."

"George!" I exclaimed, "you witnessed a landmark event in railroading," after which I extolled the significance of not only the *Zephyr* 9900 but its 1,015.4-mile dash that May 26, 1934. And then I dragged out a copy of *Classic American Streamliners* to show him photos of the 9900. As George flipped through other pages of the book, he commented, "Why, there's the Union Pacific train. . . ."

"What's that, George?"

"Why, that's the train I walked through when my folks took me to the *Century* of Progress Exhibition in Chicago in 1934," he said, pointing to a photo of the M-10000.

"You saw that, too?!" I was in awe.

"Yup. Why, I think I even got a souvenir of it that day," and he went back into his house to rummage through drawers and boxes, emerging a short time later clutching something shiny in his weathered hand.

"Here, Mike. I want you to have this. Welcome to the neighborhood." And he placed into my palm a small silvery medallion that featured a likeness of the M-10000 surrounded by the words *Union Pacific 1934 Lucky Piece.* It was indeed my lucky day.

The Burlington Northern & Santa Fe freight trains that grind past my house bear little resemblance to

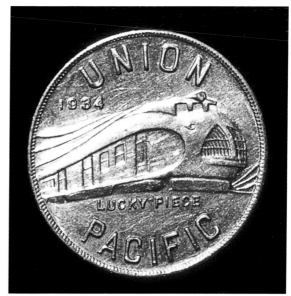

Union Pacific and Alcoa Aluminum had this aluminum medallion struck for the 1934 *Century* of Progress Exhibition, handing them out to the thousands of visitors who came to see Union Pacific's M-10000 streamliner. The reverse side reads, "A sample of the aluminum in the new Union Pacific train built by Pullman Car & Manufacturing Corp." and "ALCOA Aluminum Co. of America." George Ewing of Lee, Illinois, was one of the thousands who received the medallion as he passed through the M-10000 at the Century of Progress and 64 years later presented it as a gift to the author.

any *Zephyrs*, but when the locomotive crews wave, I think back to when the line was indeed a streamliner speedway between Chicago, the Twin Cities of St. Paul and Minneapolis, and the Pacific Northwest—a line full of trains that had been inspired by a little mercury-colored speedster named the *Zephyr* 9900 and a yellow-and-brown bullet called the M-10000.

Chapter 2

HOMETOWN STREAMLINER

Just about everyone reading this book probably grew up with a hometown streamliner, even in the Amtrak era. For many towns and cities across the nation, the streamliners that called upon them were an institution, especially between the late 1930s and the end of the 1960s.

If you grew up in Pocatello, Idaho, during that period, your hometown streamliner was Union Pacific's *City of Portland*. If you grew up in Peoria, Illinois, Rock Island's *Peoria Rocket* was your hometown

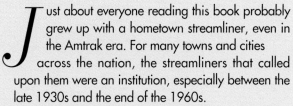

For 26 years, Illinois Central's *Land O' Corn*, in its various incarnations, called at the South Main depot in Rockford, Illinois, on its daily journeys between Lake Michigan and Iowa. In this scene from the summer of 1965, the Chicago-bound *Land O' Corn* stands at the new (1952) Rockford depot, while fathers and their sons check out the Electro-Motive diesels and discuss railroading with the white-hatted engineer. Though wearing Illinois Central colors, the lead locomotive actually belongs to Illinois Central associate Central of Georgia Railroad, which jointly operated Chicago-Florida trains with Illinois Central. On occasion, Central of Georgia locomotives were borrowed for *Land O' Corn* service.

19

UNION DEPOT,
POCATELLO, IDAHO—18

CITY OF PORTLAND

For residents of Pocatello, Idaho, Union Pacific's *City of Portland* was their hometown streamliner. From 1935 to 1971, the *City* called at Pocatello Union Depot on its way between Chicago and Oregon's largest city. This postcard dates from about 1937 and shows the second edition of the *City of Portland. Mike Schafer collection*

streamliner. Lancaster, California? Southern Pacific's *San Joaquin Daylight.* Many folks were lucky enough to live in a city that had multiple daily streamliners, like Chicago, St. Louis, or Denver.

My hometown streamliner—and we had but one—didn't have dome cars, sleepers, or parlor cars, and it didn't even have the obligatory end-of-train observation car found on many streamliners. But it was still "my" streamliner. I grew up with it, watched it die in 1967, and to this day miss it like an old friend. It was called the *Land O' Corn,* and it was Illinois Central's flagship train between Chicago and Waterloo, Iowa. Every day for 26 years, the *Land O' Corn* called at my hometown of Rockford, Illinois, twice daily, en route to Chicago and on the way back out.

The *Land O' Corn's* Formative Years

Inaugurated on October 28, 1941, the *Land O' Corn* was Illinois Central's third streamliner (after the *Green Diamond* of 1936 and the *City of Miami* of 1940), but the original version was a self-propelled "Motorailer" rather than a conventional locomotive-hauled train. This "streamlinerette," if you will, entered service on the 275-mile Chicago-Rockford-Dubuque-Waterloo route with a morning eastbound schedule and an evening westbound run, thereby

Southern Pacific's respectable and far-flung passenger service brought streamliners into numerous hometowns, including Lancaster, California, where the *San Joaquin Daylight* makes its way through town during its all-day trek between Oakland and Los Angeles. The date: May 17, 1970. On April 30, 1971, the train ended its 30-year reign in California's Central Valley. *Joe McMillan*

20

ILLINOIS CENTRAL TIME TABLE
MAIN LINE OF MID-AMERICA
CHICAGO • ROCKFORD • FREEPORT • DUBUQUE • WATERLOO • SIOUX CITY

READ DOWN — Effective April 25, 1965 — READ UP

13 Land O'Corn	11 The Hawkeye	Central Standard Time (All trains Daily)	12 The Hawkeye	14 Land O'Corn
PM	PM	(Central Station)	AM	AM
1.00	7.00	Lv......CHICAGO, ILL......Ar	7.15	11.15
f4.25	f7.30	Lv......Broadview......Lv	f6.45	a10.44
e5.06	......	Lv......Genoa......Lv	......	9.59
5.30	8.35	Ar{ ROCKFORD {Lv	5.30	9.35
5.35	8.53	Lv{ {Ar	5.18	9.35
6.10	9.23	Ar{ FREEPORT {Lv	4.50	9.03
6.13	9.38	Lv{ {Ar	4.40	8.55
d6.28	f 9.54	Lv......Lena......Lv	4.05	a8.41
6.41	10.08	Lv......Warren......Lv	a3.51	8.30
d6.48	f10.14	Lv......Apple River......Lv	f3.44	......
d6.56	......	Lv......Scales Mound......Lv	f3.33	h8.17
7.16	10.50	Lv......Galena......Lv	3.10	7.57
f7.37	......	Lv......E. Dubuque, Ill......Lv	2.46	f7.39
7.45	11.19	Ar{ DUBUQUE, IA. {Lv	2.40	7.33
7.45	11.39	Lv{ {Ar	2.20	7.33
b8.24	12.19	Lv......Dyersville......Lv	1.36	f6.55
8.44	12 48	Lv......Manchester......Lv	1.16	6.36
9.15	1.19	Lv......Independence......Lv	12.52	6.12
9.55	1.55	Ar{ WATERLOO {Lv	12.15	5.45
PM	2.20	Lv{ {Ar	12.01	AM
......	2.38	Lv......Cedar Falls......Lv	11.36	......
......	3.01	Lv......Parkersburg......Lv	11.08	......
......	3.15	Lv......Ackley......Lv	f10.52	......
......	3.45	Lv......Iowa Falls......Lv	10.38	......
......	4.25	Lv......Webster City......Lv	10.01	......
......	4.50	Ar{ FORT DODGE {Lv	9.40	......
......	5.10	Lv{ {Ar	9.25	......
......	5.38	Lv......Manson......Lv	8.47	......
......	f5.46	Lv......Pomeroy......Lv	8.34	......
......	f5.56	Lv......Fonda......Lv	f8.24	......
......	f6.05	Lv......Newell......Lv	f8.14	......
......	6.22	Lv......Storm Lake......Lv	8.00	......
......	f6.29	Lv......Alta......Lv	f7.50	......
......	f6.38	Lv......Aurelia......Lv	f7.40	......
......	6.55	Lv......Cherokee......Lv	7.28	......
......	f7.07	Lv......Cleghorn......Lv	f7.12	......
......	f7.12	Lv......Marcus......Lv	f7.07	......
......	f7.22	Lv......Remsen......Lv	f6.57	......
......	7.40	Lv......Le Mars......Lv	6.45	......
......	8.30	Ar....SIOUX CITY, IA....Lv	6.10	......
	AM		PM	

Reference Notes

a—Stops to receive or discharge revenue passengers to or from Rockford and beyond.
b—Stops to discharge revenue passengers from Freeport and points east.
d—Stops to discharge revenue passengers from Rockford and East.
e—Stops to discharge revenue passengers from Chicago, also to receive revenue passengers for scheduled stops Dubuque and beyond.
f—Stops on flag.
h—Stops to receive revenue passengers for Rockford and east thereof.

EQUIPMENT
Nos. 11 and 12—The Hawkeye
CHICAGO—WATERLOO—SIOUX CITY

Sleepers		Car No. West	East
Chicago—Sioux City			
6 Sections, 6 Roomettes, 4 Double Bedrooms		111	122

Reclining Seat Coaches: Chicago—Sioux City

Nos. 13 and 14—Land O' Corn
COACH STREAMLINER—CHICAGO—WATERLOO
Reclining Seat Coaches   Diner Lounge Service

No. 70—Rand McNally   15M—4-25-1965

A pocket timetable from 1965 shows the Land O' Corn's *longtime traditional "shoppers' schedule," which allowed for an afternoon in Chicago's Loop district.* Mike Schafer collection

offering an afternoon of shopping in downtown Chicago. The new *Land O' Corn* complemented its sister trains on the Chicago-Iowa route, notably the *Hawkeye*, the *Iowan*, and the *Sinnissippi*.

Unfortunately, mechanical breakdowns plagued the new *Land O' Corn*, and then on February 18, 1942, a semi pulled into its path at Plato Center, Illinois. The train was wrecked, killing engineer D. H. Sullivan and injuring some two dozen passengers. Frustrated with the Motorailer's performance, Illinois Central returned the train to its builder, American Car & Foundry (ACF), which in turn rebuilt and sold it to the New York, Susquehanna & Western. Left without substitute streamlined equipment, Illinois Central simply made the *Land O' Corn* a conventional steam-powered heavyweight train for the remainder of the World War II years.

Like many other railroads, Illinois Central resumed its streamlining program after the war, placing a twofold order for streamlined equipment: part with carbuilder Pullman-Standard and part with its own Burnside Shops in Chicago. Pullman-Standard would provide new-from-the-ground-up rolling stock while Burnside rebuilt 1920s-era heavyweight steel cars into streamlined and semistreamlined rolling stock. Most of this new and rebuilt equipment came on line in 1947, allowing IC to convert a number of trains to streamliner status or upgrade pre-existing streamliners. Thus, the *Land O' Corn* was reborn as a streamliner on February 12, 1947. In this reincarnation it featured a new 2,000-horsepower Electro-Motive E7A passenger diesel, three Pullman-Standard reclining-seat coaches, a café-lounge car, two more coaches, and—westbound only between Chicago and Freeport, Illinois—a full dining car to accommodate heavy dinnertime patronage out of Chicago.

Early *Land O' Corn* Memories

I appeared on the scene early in 1949 and can recall encounters with the *Land O' Corn* as early as 1952. For Rockfordians, the ritual was to head for Illinois Central's Main Street depot downtown to

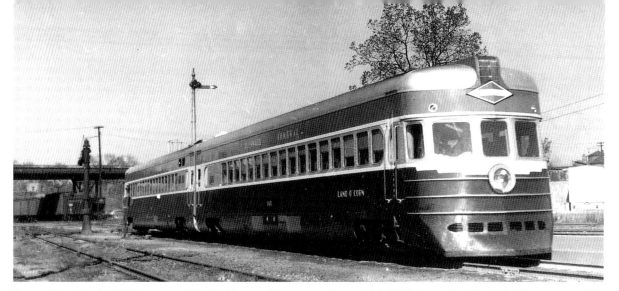

The original Illinois Central *Land O' Corn* coasts into the Rockford depot, possibly on its inaugural run in the fall of 1941. American Car and Foundry built the two-car train, which accommodated 111 passengers and had a dining area featuring two booths and a lunch counter. The train was painted blue, red, and cream while the interior was done in green, red, yellow, and silver, supposedly representing the colors of a corn plant. *T. V. Maguire, Mike Schafer collection via Jim Scribbins*

watch the *Land O' Corn* roll in on its high-speed evening run from Chicago. My family's ritual was a little different. My mother occasionally shopped after supper at Rockford Standard Furniture Company, hard against the Illinois Central main line on Rockford's east side. Rather than tag along with Mom through the store, my sister and I would stand at the huge picture windows that faced the tracks. With great anticipation, we carefully watched out the window at the black-and-white-striped crossing gates protecting 11th Street. Our patience was always duly rewarded: The gates' red lights would illuminate, the gates would lower, and—air-chime horn blaring—the *Land O' Corn* would make its grand sweep into town, its oscillating Mars warning light painting the facade of the furniture store. For this four-year-old already fascinated by trains, this was ecstasy of the highest order.

My first ride on a train was not on the *Land O' Corn* but in Rockford's denizen of the dawn, the *Hawkeye*. On the day after Thanksgiving 1953, my mother, sister, and I rode the *Hawkeye* into Chicago for a day of shopping and sightseeing. This became a family ritual that always included a stop at the king of department stores, Marshall Field's, whose astonishing toy department (complete with American Flyer,

Lionel, and Marx electric train displays, of course) was one of the Seven Wonders of the Midwest.

We returned home that evening on the *Land O' Corn*, which introduced me to high-speed railroading. The 86 miles separating Central Station on Chicago's lakefront and the Rockford depot was carded at 90 minutes flat. This run included some 15 miles of congested Chicago Terminal District tracks and two intermediate station stops, at suburban Hines (later Broadview) and Genoa. That meant No. 13 had to average nearly a mile a minute to stay on time. To accomplish this, a *Land O' Corn* engineer later told me, sprints of 90 to 100 miles per hour were required west of the suburbs. In any event, I do indeed remember a speedy ride back to Rockford that evening, as well as my mother's grumbling about the "crack-the-whip" ride in the last car, to which we were assigned.

I remember a later trip to Chicago, again with my mother and sister, when we rode the *Land O' Corn* in. The train was jam-packed and had extra cars that day, but we found window seats as the *Corn* got under way. My sister and I shrieked as the train roared onto the bridge over the Rock River east of the station. All previous trips over this span had been

Levi Markely was a veteran conductor on the Illinois Central between Chicago and Dubuque, Iowa. His congenial presence was a familiar part of the *Land O' Corn* experience for regular riders, and he was known to have supplied a freebie trip or two to this book's author out on a *Land O' Corn* joy ride.

during darkness, so this was an amazing new vista for us. This bridge has no railings, and from a passenger car one could look straight down into the water. My face pressed against the window, my sister shoved against me, insisting she was going to tip the train into the water. Laughter and more shrieking ensued.

Once in Chicago, we made the obligatory Loop stops at Field's and Carson Pirie Scott. Interestingly, one of the toys I got that day was a little wind-up plastic version of the General Motors/Pullman-

Standard *Train of Tomorrow* streamliner—a train I would be writing about in books some 40 years later. I wish I still had that toy; it's probably worth a small fortune today.

So captivated was I by the *Land O' Corn* that, as a budding young artist, I often drew pictures of it with chocolate brown, orange, and yellow Crayolas. I sent one of my elaborate drawings of the *Land O' Corn* to Rockford's WTVO television station, which aired it on the evening kid's show right after the *Crusader Rabbit* cartoon.

My "Freedom Years" with the *Land O' Corn*

By 1964, I had achieved freedom to travel with other friends and without parental supervision, so we began making forays into Chicago for purposes of train-watching. I remember one summer trip in 1964 when a buddy and I spent the afternoon traipsing through all the major downtown Chicago railroad terminals to see arriving and departing streamliners. We began at North Western Terminal and then, in succession, marched to Union Station, Grand Central Station, La Salle Street Station, and Dearborn Station, witnessing the likes of Milwaukee Road's *Morning Hiawatha*, Burlington's *Morning Zephyr* and *Empire Builder*, Baltimore & Ohio's *Capitol Limited*, New York Central's *New England States*, Santa Fe's *San Francisco Chief*, and the Wabash *Blue Bird*.

Our final stop was Central Station for the 6 P.M. departure of the *Land O' Corn* back home. The temperature that afternoon in the Loop was at least 190 degrees—or so it felt—and the air-conditioned *Corn* stood like an oasis in the oppressive heat of the train shed. Exhausted, dehydrated, and gritty, we clambered aboard, opening the pneumatic door to enter the coach and feel the blast of chilly air. Ah!

Next order of business: slake thirst. We relocated to the café-lounge and ordered two Cokes. As No. 13 eased out of the depot, the sharply dressed attendant delivered two tall glasses—emblazoned with the Illinois Central diamond logo, of course—brimming with chunks of clear ice and two cans (steel, back then) of

Coke. Sipping the most wonderful icy Coca-Cola I can ever remember, we watched as our train negotiated the complex tracks leading away from the lakefront. As the *Corn* slowed for 21st Street Junction, we saw one more streamliner: Monon's *Thoroughbred* from Louisville, cruising by on nearby Chicago & Western Indiana tracks. Six Cokes and 80 minutes later, we were cruising into the outskirts of Rockford, having logged yet another trip on the *Land O' Corn*.

By the mid-1960s, the *Land O' Corn*'s makeup had changed somewhat. The train was handling a respectable amount of mail and express carried in baggage cars and on "Flexi-Van" flatcars. The 1947 coaches had been supplanted with secondhand streamlined coaches acquired in 1960 from the Chicago & Eastern Illinois Railroad. These smooth-riding cars were built for C&EI's short-lived streamliners, the *Whippoorwill* and the *Meadowlark*. The regularly assigned café-lounge now, car 4150, was an elderly veteran in disguise. Built in 1912, the car was modernized in 1935 and again after the war. Illinois Central, the ultimate frugal Midwestern carrier, got a

The westbound *Land O' Corn* eases through Buckbee Siding on Rockford's east side while Council Bluffs (Iowa)–Chicago meat train CC-6 roars east on the main line in June 1967. Partially visible in the background is the now-abandoned Rockford Standard Furniture building where, as young tykes in the early 1950s, the author and his sister used to stand in the main floor display windows to watch for the evening *Land O' Corn* sweep in from Chicago.

Growing Up with Katy

By Mike McBride

By the mid-1960s, only one streamliner of Chicago & North Western's once-impressive fleet remained on the old double-track Overland Route though my hometown of Dixon, Illinois: The *Kate Shelley "400,"* train Nos. 1 and 2. Inaugurated in 1955 as a Chicago-Boone, Iowa, run, the *Kate Shelley "400"* was named for an Iowa heroine who saved the lives of an engine crew when a bridge collapsed under their locomotive during a storm in long-ago 1881.

"The *Katy*," as the train was locally known, was a little streamliner: an E-series Electro-Motive passenger diesel, two or three coaches, and a diner-lounge. It connected Chicago with the small towns that dotted C&NW's main line across northern Illinois. Eastbound the train called at Dixon at 7:13 A.M.; westbound out of Chicago at 6:38 P.M. People would drive to the Dixon depot after supper to pick up friends or relatives or just to watch the train come in. In a small town where nothing much ever happened, the train's arrival was a celebration of sorts.

In our high school years, a couple of friends and I would ride the train into Chicago for a day, or sometimes we'd go just to Rochelle, 23 miles and 21 minutes east of Dixon. There, at the crossing of the C&NW and Burlington's Chicago–Twin Cities main line, we watched trains. It was a great way to spend a Saturday.

One Rochelle trip stands out in my memory. April 13, 1965, had been a good day photographing the parade of trains past Rochelle tower, which guarded the crossing. At sunset we packed up our cameras, thanked the tower's leverman, and trudged over to the C&NW depot for *Katy*'s 6:17 P.M. departure. Number 1 arrived on time, and we took our seats in one of the shiny yellow *"400"* coaches. By now it was dark, and we relaxed as the lights of Rochelle slipped silently past our window.

We talked of going to the dining car for hot chocolate after the conductor lifted our tickets. The regular conductor on the *Katy* was a distinguished-looking gentleman who appeared to be at least 100 years old to us kids. A veteran of many years and tens

Chicago & North Western's *Kate Shelley "400"* was the new hometown streamliner of Dixon, Illinois, after Union Pacific's *City* trains were moved from the Chicago & North Western to the Milwaukee Road between Chicago and Omaha in 1955. On a lazy summer evening in 1965, *"Katy"* stops at Dixon. *Mike McBride*

of thousands of rail-miles, he swayed gently with the motion of the train as he punched our tickets. He was a friendly, soft-spoken man, and we made some small talk with him. As a joke, one of our group asked if we could ride in the cab of the locomotive. "Well," he said, "only the engineer can give you permission to do that. Go up and ask him." We stared at each other in disbelief for but a second, and then the three of us rose in unison and headed forward.

The sight that greeted us—the back end of 2,000 horsepower's worth of bouncing diesel—as we opened the door of the lead coach almost changed our minds. To get to the cab we had to make our way through the engine room of the rocketing locomotive. We opened and cautiously entered the locomotive's rear door.

It was dark and extremely noisy. We inched sideways along an oily and very narrow walkway with the hot, roaring diesel prime movers just inches from our sides. A few 15-watt bulbs in the blackness somewhere overhead provided barely enough light to see. To keep from being thrown off our feet by the rough ride, we clung to the car body's iron framework. Finally, we exited through a small door and into the locomotive's cab. The engine crew was startled by our appearance, but they allowed us to stay.

Our cab ride was high adventure to say the least. The noisy cab was heavy with the pleasant railroady smell of oil and hot motors. We talked with the fireman, watched the engineer blow the whistle for crossings, and noted the speedometer needle touching 90 miles per hour. We met an eastbound freight near Nachusa, and the noise of its passing sounded like an explosion. Soon after, we felt the brakes grabbing hard for the train's descent on Dixon Hill into the station. We climbed down the locomotive ladder and waved from the depot platform as the engineer whistled a highball in response to the conductor's lantern signal. It had been one heck of a ride home!

Riding trains was always fun, but this trip was a real thrill. It was all part of growing up in rural northern Illinois, an area served by "our streamliner," the *Kate Shelley "400."*

lot of miles out of this and other similar oldies that had been heavily upgraded by Burnside Shops. Imagine, a 50-plus-year-old car masquerading as a modern streamliner diner!

By 1965, all was not blue sky and puffy clouds as rumblings surfaced about IC discontinuing the *Land O' Corn.* The 1955 opening of the Northwest Tollway severely eroded discretionary Chicago-Rockford rail travel during the ensuing decade. (As a connector to other Chicago-based trains and because of its heavy mail and express business, the *Hawkeye* was less affected.) Surprisingly, Illinois Central backpedaled its threats and instead of discontinuing the train, made—at the behest of the U.S. Postal Service—what was called an "Interim Order Schedule" adjustment in the spring of 1966.

In this incarnation, the eastbound run remained on its traditional schedule with a noontime arrival in Chicago, but the westbound now departed Chicago in the morning. At the same time, Illinois Central downgraded the train by replacing the café-lounge car with box lunches, assigning mostly rebuilt heavyweight coaches, and lengthening Chicago-Rockford running times by as much as 18 minutes.

One good thing that came out of the new *Land O' Corn* format, at least for those of us with a bent for train-riding, was that the revised schedule allowed for a quick midday round-trip joy ride to Genoa, a flagstop station 25 miles east of Rockford. You'd leave Rockford at 10:10 A.M. on the eastbound "Can O' Corn" (as we were now wanton to call it), arrive at Genoa at 10:40 A.M., board the westbound *Corn* at 11:22 A.M., and be back in Rockford by noon. A flagstop, by the way, is one where the train only stops on special signal from the depot agent.

Although one might ponder what to do in Genoa for 45 minutes at a shoe box–size depot on the outskirts of town, that was not a problem for me. One of my best friends, Mike McBride of Dixon, Illinois, happened to be a new IC employee assigned to Genoa as the "relief" man for the regular agent/operator. And herein begins one of my

favorite *Land O' Corn* tales, known throughout northern Illinois as "The Great Genoa *Cap*er."

On a blustery Saturday in the fall of 1966, I rode No. 14 to Genoa to visit McBride. Time slipped by quickly as we yakked inside the depot's tiny office, and before long I happened to glance out the bay window down the tracks toward Chicago. A spot of headlight on the horizon told me that No. 13 was out of Burlington.

"Uh, McBride," I said, "you do know this is a flag stop for No. 13, don't you? I can't miss the *Land O' Corn* back to Rockford as I gotta be at work this afternoon."

"Uh-oh," he said, panic rising in his voice, "now how in the hell do I flag a passenger train?!"

It suddenly became clear that he had never had to flag a passenger train before. For that matter, neither had I. Logic dictated my response: "McBride, just wave that red flag that's laying over there on the desk."

He hesitated, muttering something about there being another color flag to signal a passenger pickup, but the red flag was the only one we saw. Meanwhile No. 13 was hurtling nearer to Genoa. McBride grabbed the red flag and ran outside.

When the red flag went up, the engineer responded with a single blast of the horn and applied the emergency brakes. We were about to find out that a red flag is just as effective in stopping a train as a red block signal, and railroad rule books across the land demand that a train may not pass a red signal under any circumstance.

Sounds of screeching steel and brakeshoe smoke were everywhere, and—sure enough—the locomotives ground to a halt at the red flag held by the now-trembling McBride. In nano seconds, the conductor was on the ground and running forward along the train. Lightning struck and area wildlife scampered for cover.

"What the hell is going on here?" the conductor demanded. "There'd better be a damn good reason for stopping this train with a red flag!" (An acceptable reason would have been a gaping chasm in the track a mile deep just beyond the depot.)

Leaning out the cab window and door, the fireman and engineer hounded in unison.

McBride, somewhat meekly, replied, "Uh, I have a passenger for you for, uh . . . Rockford. . . ."

"YOU WHAT?"

Obviously, the conductor was not amused. "Don't you know that you use the green-and-white flag combination to signal a stop for passengers?" He was right, of course. The green and white flags would have allowed the engineer to roll past the flags and easily stop the train with the coaches in front of the depot. As it turned out, the green and white flags had fallen behind the file cabinet, which McBride wouldn't discover for several more days. In any event, once the commotion subsided, the train pulled ahead, stopping with the coaches in front of me. I (also somewhat meekly) boarded.

When we arrived back in Rockford, the conductor rushed into the depot office where he filed a report about the incident with the dispatcher, trainmaster, his union steward, and probably the U.S. attorney general. McBride was called on the carpet, and to this day, even though he hasn't worked for a railroad for years, he carries green and white flags on his person at all times, just in case. As for me, I was glad I didn't have to ride No. 13 any farther than Rockford that day. The flat wheels resulting from the emergency stop made the ride awfully noisy and bumpy.

The End

Illinois Central's experiment with the *Land O' Corn* was unsuccessful, and as 1967 unfolded, the railroad posted NOTICE OF PROPOSED DISCONTINUANCE

A shortage of E-series passenger diesels led Illinois Central to "passengerize" several of its Electro-Motive GP-series freight locomotives, such as the pair bucking a snowstorm while heading out of Rockford for Chicago in December 1966. These diesels were equipped with steam generators for train heating and four were geared for high-speed travel—83 miles per hour—so they could maintain passenger schedules. They were long a common sight on all Iowa Division passenger trains after dieselization.

OF SERVICE placards at all stations for trains 13 and 14. Formal application had been made with the Interstate Commerce Commission to, ahem, "can" the *Corn.* We focused on photographing and riding it as much as feasible before the projected end of service on August 5, 1967.

There was no way I was going to miss the last runs of my beloved *Land O' Corn* on August 5. Alas, about 9 A.M. on that day, I received a phone call at work from friend Jim Boyd who lived in an apartment next to the Illinois Central tracks and who also was going to photograph the last runs.

"Hey Schaf," he said with an uneasy tone, "I woke up to see a mighty strange-looking *Hawkeye* leave for Chicago early this morning. Attached to the end of the train were two locomotives, a bunch of Flexi-Vans and baggage cars, and a couple of coaches."

I felt the blood drain from my face when it began to sink in what had happened: We misinterpreted the discontinuance notices, all of which said the train would be discontinued *effective* August 5. That is to say, the trains would no longer exist as of that date. They made their final runs the day before. Jim had seen the *Land O' Corn's* equipment from the previous day's last westbound run being deadheaded from Waterloo back to Chicago. I never got to say "so long" to my steel-wheeled friend of 18 years.

Genoa, Illinois, location of "The Great Genoa Caper" described in the text, was a flag stop for Iowa Division passenger trains 60 miles west of Chicago and 25 miles east of Rockford. The westbound *Land O' Corn,* behind a single locomotive, apparently has Genoa passengers on this bucolic evening in July 1958. Forty-one years later, the little wooden depot here still stood, an abandoned and forlorn reminder of a finer era of rail travel. *Howard Patrick*

Chapter 3

STREAMLINER MEMORIES EAST AND WEST

*T*ravelers railing their way between America's heartland and the Atlantic seaboard had an unparalleled number of streamliner options. Heading from Boston to St. Louis? New York Central's *Southwestern Limited* was highly recommended. Travelers destined to Virginia's Hampton Roads region from the Midwest could choose between Norfolk & Western's *Powhatan Arrow* or Chesapeake & Ohio's *George Washington*. And as for Chicago–New York, no fewer than six railroads at one time or another offered streamliners between the largest and then second-largest U.S. metro areas.

Pennsylvania GG1 electric 4925 is in command of a shiny-clean Chicago-bound *Broadway Limited*, marching grandly away from the Newark (New Jersey) stop on a steamy summer evening in June 1968. Although the Penn Central merger had occurred only months earlier, the train still looked much like a Blue Ribbon streamliner of the late, great Pennsylvania Railroad. By this time, however, the *Broadway's* running mate, the *General*, had been discontinued and its coaches and Washington-Chicago cars added to the *Broadway*. The Washington cars will join the train at Harrisburg, Pennsylvania.

NEW YORK CENTRAL'S NEW

Southwestern Limited

PULLMAN DREAMLINER
AND COACH STREAMLINER,
ALL IN ONE NEW STAIN-
LESS STEEL DIESELINER!

The preferred time slot for travel between mid-America and the East Coast was a late-afternoon departure from either region with arrival at the other the following morning. So popular was this scheduling that New York Central, Pennsylvania Railroad, and Baltimore & Ohio—the chief competitors in this market—operated multiple overnighters to accommodate demand.

Central's premier New York–Chicago flagship, of course, was the world-class *20th Century Limited*. The *Century* was supplemented by another exclusive all-Pullman train, the *Commodore Vanderbilt*, while the *Pacemaker* catered to the increasingly popular coach trade in the overnight Chicago–New York market.

New York Central's *Southwestern*, shown leaving St. Louis Union Station on August 4, 1966, was the premier train on Central's New York–Cleveland–St. Louis route and for a time also had a Boston section. Despite a national airline strike at the time of this photo, the *Southwestern* was now carrying only a single sleeping car and two reclining-seat coaches. A buffet-lounge will be added to the train at Indianapolis. The magazine ad from circa 1950 touts the newly streamlined *Southwestern Limited*.

A contestant in the Chicago–New York (via Hoboken, New Jersey) streamliner parade for only a brief period—1964 to 1967—Erie Lackawanna's extended *Phoebe Snow* (it had been a Hoboken-Buffalo train for most of its life) nonetheless garnered high praise for friendly service and excellent cuisine. *Phoebe* is shown exiting Chicago on a July evening in 1965. EL's long running times (about 24 hours versus about 16 for competitors New York Central and Pennsylvania Railroad), lightly populated route, and ferry/subway transfer to reach Manhattan kept the carrier a distant third in the market.

In like manner, Pennsy had its all-Pullman *Broadway Limited*, complemented by the all-Pullman *General*; coach passengers rode the *Trail Blazer*. In 1951, the *General* and the *Trail Blazer* were combined, an early indication of a slip in traffic that would only increase.

Pennsy's Four-Star *General*

My opportunity to ride Pennsy's *General* came in the fall of 1967. A buddy of mine and I had traveled from Chicago to Lima, Ohio, on the Pennsylvania Railroad's dog-eared *Pennsylvania Limited* to attend an historical society convention. With the convention over, we needed an early morning train back out of Lima. The westbound *General*'s 6:01 A.M. departure fit the bill and provided a ride aboard something a little classier than the rockin'-and-rollin' heavyweight coach we had endured on the *Pennsylvania Limited*.

You can't talk about Chicago–New York streamliners without mentioning the world's most-famous train, New York Central's *20th Century Limited.* The eastbound *Century* is only 7 miles into its 961-mile overnight speed run to Manhattan on this fall evening at Englewood station in 1965, but we can presume passengers are already sipping liquid Manhattans in the train's sleeper-lounge-observation car. *Jim Boyd*

We had briefly considered the *Broadway Limited* until we determined that we didn't have the resources for Pullman accommodations. Aside from that was another critical factor: the *Broadway* didn't stop at Lima. Even in 1967, the *Broadway* maintained a *Limited*-stop schedule, with the *General* handling more-local travel duties.

Tickets in hand, we positioned ourselves with a klatch of other passengers on the platform of the joint PRR-B&O station in predawn darkness. Off to the east came the distinct trumpeting of Pennsy multi-chime air horns. The *General* was dead on time.

An impressively long train rushed into the station, pausing impatiently as all were ushered aboard. The *General* was under way before we even found a pair of bulkhead seats in a nearly full coach. We settled in and immediately took note of two things: speed and comfort. Though only minutes out of Lima, the *General* was already blazing along at what we estimated to be about 90 miles per hour, and yet there was nary a pitch or shudder from our coach. The *General* was carded at 3 hours and 45 minutes on the 207.5-mile run between Lima and Chicago Union Station, which meant maintaining an average speed of just over 55 miles per hour. Sound easy? Not when you take into consideration scheduled stops at Fort Wayne, Warsaw, Plymouth, Valparaiso, and Gary, Indiana, and Englewood, Illinois. We began to understand the *General*'s expeditious nature as Pennsy's bright position-light signals blipped past our window, lulling us into doze mode.

When rays of morning sun began to stream into the coach, the steward briskly marched through our car announcing, "First call to breakfast." We obliged. On today's Amtrak long-distance trains, such an announcement often draws a stampede to the diner, but such was not the case on the *General*. In the

Even in its twilight years, the *Capitol Limited* was a first-rate effort on behalf of Baltimore & Ohio. Though slightly battered, the locomotives in this 1971 scene of No. 6 leaving North Western Terminal in Chicago lead a sparkling-clean set of equipment. B&O prided itself in service quality, right up to the end on May 1, 1971.

THE GENERAL

FASTER than ever

BETTER than ever

NEW YORK–CHICAGO 16 HOURS

FEATURING NEW ALL-PRIVATE-ROOM SLEEPING CARS

The *General* is on its home stretch into Chicago on July 16, 1966. Three Electro-Motive E-series passenger diesels have No. 49 approaching the portal of Union Station (behind the photographer) right on time at 8:45 A.M. Also on time and on the heels of the *General* is the *Broadway Limited*, with a 9 A.M. arrival at Chicago's Union Station. The brochure for the upgraded 1949 *General* spotlights its new sleepers, part of a huge order for new cars from American Car & Foundry, Pullman-Standard, and Budd. *Brochure collection of Joe Welsh*

1960s, dining car fare was perceived to be ultra-expensive (it often was) and many riders shunned the dining experience as delightful as it was.

Our train featured a twin-unit diner, consisting of a kitchen-dormitory car mated with a high-capacity dining car. The steward seated us at a table near the portal between the two cars, and we wrote down our orders for traditional bacon-and-egg breakfasts. The portal contained treadle-operated pneumatic sliding doors separating the dining room in our car from the kitchen in the adjacent car, and we had fun watching the waiter dash back and forth between the two cars with trays of food, usually hitting the treadle just right to part the doors while anticipating the speeding train's jostles.

The scrambled eggs and bacon arrived in modest portions served on Pennsylvania Railroad's "Mountain Laurel" china. The milk I got had soured, so I sent it back in exchange for coffee. On his way back to the kitchen, the waiter misstepped the treadle, tripping into the doors and sending the carton of sour milk and its contents flying. He spoke not a word, but gathered himself up and went about his duties. I felt bad for sending the milk back.

After breakfast, we strolled into the adjacent lounge car, a square-end broiler-lounge observation car built by Pennsy's Juniata Shops (Altoona, Pennsylvania) in 1947 for the *Trail Blazer* and the New York–St. Louis *Jeffersonian*. We sat in this nearly empty car until the *General* was cruising down the 8-mile home stretch between Englewood and Chicago Union Station for an on-time 8:45 A.M. arrival. We tarried in the Union Station concourse long enough to watch the *Broadway Limited* which, running non-stop between Fort Wayne and Englewood, had closed the gap with our train and was now making its 9 A.M. arrival. Number 29 rolled to a halt on the opposite side of the platform, at which our *General*

was still standing. Even in their slightly tattered, weathered state, the Tuscan red locomotives of the *General* and the *Broadway* loomed regal in the dim confines of Union Station, and I got goose bumps staring at Pennsy's two most-important flagships flanking a stream of detraining travelers.

Some three months later the *General* was gone. It turned out to be the only train of Pennsy's famed "Blue Ribbon" streamliner fleet that I would have the opportunity to ride. On February 1, 1968, Pennsylvania Railroad and New York Central merged to form Penn Central, ending an era once marked by intense passenger competition in the Midwest–East Coast market.

Outside of the Chicago-Florida market, Baltimore & Ohio was the only non-Amtrak Chicago–East Coast carrier to boast dome-car service, first on its all-coach *Columbian* and then later on the *Capitol* when the two trains were combined in 1958. From aboard these glass-enclosed upper decks (this is a Pullman-Standard dome coach on the *Cap* in 1965), passengers could behold the beauty of the Potomac River valley. *Bob Johnston*

Author Mike Schafer (right, in blue shirt) and an unidentified seat mate enjoy dinner—served on Baltimore & Ohio Centenary blue china—aboard the *Capitol Limited* just a week before its April 30, 1971, finale. Little did the author know at that time that 10 years hence he would be enjoying such repasts again on a revived *Capitol Limited*. *Ron Lundstrom*

A "Capitol" Idea

A funny thing happened on the way to Amtrak's 1971 startup. During the shake-out of the late 1960s that decimated most intercity streamliners on Midwest-Atlantic routes, the "odd man out" wound up a winner. The "odd man" in this case was the venerable Baltimore & Ohio, America's oldest (1827) common-carrier railroad.

Long the underdog in the Midwest–East Coast market, B&O was hampered by its circuitous (and geographically the most rugged) route between the two regions, running between Chicago and Jersey City via Pittsburgh, Washington, D.C., Baltimore, and Philadelphia. In 1958, the railroad retrenched its intercity passenger trains from Jersey City to Baltimore, conceding the Chicago–New York and St.

Louis–New York markets to the Pennsylvania Railroad and New York Central. In its new role, B&O focused on the Midwest-Washington market, emerging as a respectable alternative to Pennsy's Midwest-Washington trains.

Like just about every railroad in the 1960s, Baltimore & Ohio then—now closely allied with Chesapeake & Ohio—had to address a serious decline in passenger revenues by dropping some runs and consolidating others. But unlike some of their contemporaries, B&O/C&O made a concerted effort to operate their remaining trains with dignity and even a dose of panache and innovation, including current-release onboard movies.

The big shake-out accelerated as the 1960s wound down. Newly formed Penn Central had no interest in maintaining a quality passenger network and began downgrading its intercity trains. Although former-Pennsy flagships such as the *Cincinnati Limited* and *Broadway Limited* survived, they were but hollow, shabby vestiges of their former glory, reflective of their bankrupt parent. (Penn Central declared bankruptcy on June 1, 1970. At the time, it was the largest corporate bankruptcy in American history.) So, as the 1970s dawned, there remained but two truly respectable flagships in the Midwest–East Coast market: C&O/B&O's Washington–St. Louis/Louisville/Detroit *George Washington* and B&O's Washington-Chicago *Capitol Limited* (the latter having become arguably the finest streamliner operating between Chicago and the East Coast).

As part of a soirée to ride several trains to be cut by the impending Amtrak ax on May 1, 1971, a fellow railroad aficionado and I chose to start our journey on the *Capitol Limited*. Despite the crush under way as people across America sought passage aboard doomed trains, we were able to secure a bedroom out of Chicago to Washington on Friday, April 23, 1971.

We boarded our sparkling clean streamliner at North Western Terminal (B&O and C&O having moved out of Chicago's Grand Central Station in 1969), pleased to discover our bedroom was located in sleeper-lounge-observation car *Dana*, operating mid-train. Number 6 had two E-series passenger diesels, two coaches, the *Dana*, a regular sleeper, and a tavern lunch-counter-lounge observation car. At 3:50 P.M., the *Capitol* eased away from the bumping post and began its hour-long convoluted ramble through the industrial backwaters of Chicagoland. Once away from the

During a station stop in Ohio after dinner, the *Capitol* conductor and the car attendant for sleeper-lounge-observation car *Dana* (behind the two men) pose with their train.

Gary, Indiana, stop at 5:03 P.M., the *Capitol* began to gallop across the Hoosier farmlands.

B&O was perhaps best known for fine dining, and we were not disappointed. For me, this repast on the famous *Capitol* was an event, and accordingly I donned a dark blue shirt and blue-and-gold tie (in keeping with B&O colors) for our visit to the "Iron Horse Tavern," as C&O/B&O billed its food and lounge service. The limited kitchen area of the diner-lounge observation car—built by the Budd Company in 1948 for C&O's planned Cincinnati-Virginia *Chessie* streamliner—did not hamper the chef's ability to produce excellent chicken dinners for us, all served on B&O's classic Centenary blue china.

After dinner we retreated to the lounge area of our sleeper, joining a crowd of passengers in the throes of revelry, thanks in part to the imbibing of alcohol and to a budding folksinger who had brought his guitar along for the ride. The sing-a-longs and such helped mask what we felt was the only flaw of the trip: rough track.

Nighttime slumber was interrupted briefly by an awesome view of Pittsburgh sliding quietly past the bedroom window. B&O's *Capitol* skirted the Steel *City* on Pittsburgh & Lake Erie tracks on the opposite side of the Youghiogheny River, affording a spectacular vista of Pittsburgh's impressive skyline and dragon-fire steel mills.

We awoke at daybreak to a gait noticeably more leisure from the prior night's dash across Indiana and Ohio. Now well ensconced in the Appalachian Mountains, the *Capitol* was nosing first this way then that through curves and tunnels while skirting cool and leafy streams laced with spring

One particularly animated passenger aboard the *Capitol* leads fellow travelers in a lively sing-a-long in the lounge section of the *Dana*. The lounge was soon all laughter and (attempted) singing. Another passenger followed suit with a guitar on this April 23, 1971, train trip.

green foliage. Following an extended stop at the rambling B&O depot and Cumberland Hotel in Cumberland, Maryland, we vied for breakfast seating.

The cruise along the historic Potomac River and the stop at Harpers Ferry, West Virginia, where the *Capitol* crossed the Potomac into Maryland proved to be the scenic highlights of the journey. All too soon, No. 5 was backing into Washington Union Station for its 10 A.M. arrival, and a memorable ride was over. One week later, the final *Capitol Limited*s arrived at their respective destinations—Chicago and Washington—as Amtrak began its limited operations.

Chapter 4

WESTERN TRANSCONS, WESTERN RECOLLECTIONS

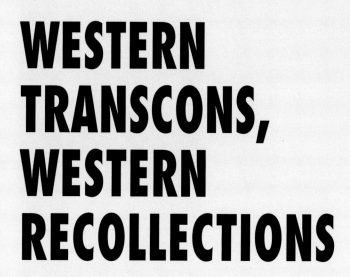

*T*he vast expanse that is the American West was perhaps the ultimate domain for streamliners. Glorious mountain scenery and sprawling deserts beckoned travelers to put down their magazines and head for the Vista-Domes or observation cars to experience unparalleled lessons in American history and geography.

Every day during the streamliner era, famous and not-so-famous transcontinental flyers originated

A pioneer in streamliner operation, Union Pacific created a comprehensive fleet of *City*-themed streamliners that drew accolades from travelers from the mid-1930s until Amtrak stilled most of the yellow-and-gray trains in May 1971. Just weeks before the end, the combined westbound *City of Los Angeles*/San Francisco/ Portland/Kansas *City*—four trains in one—descends Sherman Hill in Wyoming high country. At Green River, Wyoming, the *City of Portland* cars will be split from the train to head northwest, while at Ogden, Utah, the remaining section will be split for Los Angeles and Oakland, California. Most of rival Santa Fe's trains were concentrated on the somewhat sparsely populated Los Angeles–Chicago route that in part followed famed, old U.S. Route 66 while Union Pacific *City trains* tapped Chicago, Kansas City, Los Angeles, San Francisco, Omaha, Denver, St. Louis, and Portland.

The boarding of transcontinental streamliners at major cities was usually handled in an orderly fashion to ensure that everyone was in their proper seat or room. At Chicago Union Station in 1971, coach and sleeping-car passengers funnel through the Milwaukee Road check-in desks prior to boarding the West Coast–bound combined *City* trains. Milwaukee Road ferried Union Pacific's *City* trains between Chicago and Omaha. *Bob Johnston*

at Chicago, St. Louis, Kansas *City*, and New Orleans for exotic destinations that rang with excitement and adventure: San Francisco, Los Angeles (Hollywood in particular), Portland, Seattle, Salt Lake *City*, Denver, Albuquerque. These were places made accessible in the comfort of reclining-seat coaches, private rooms, and chic lounge cars of such trains as Great Northern's *Western Star*, Southern Pacific's *Sunset Limited*, Union Pacific's *City of Los Angeles*, Santa Fe's *San Francisco Chief*, and Rock Island's *Rocky Mountain Rocket*.

Santa Fe: Best in Show

It is in this writer's humble opinion that the award for "Best in Show" in streamliner operation goes to fabled Atchison, Topeka & Santa Fe. In terms of equipment maintenance, food quality, reliability, and just plain impeccable service, few railroads approached the level of Santa Fe. For example, how many railroads went to the trouble of touching up the paint on the interior walls of their cars every time a train laid over for servicing at a terminal endpoint? Santa Fe did.

Another important criteria: train themes. Santa Fe's handling of a Native American motif to its streamliner fleet bestowed great dignity to the American Southwest Indian. As an artist and a descendant in part of Native Americans, I was

A World War II–era tinted postcard illustrates the appeal of "streamlining through sunny California." The new Electro-Motive E6A locomotive leading this train (possibly on the *El Capitan*) through concocted scenery has a special headlight shroud to reduce upward headlight glare. During the war, locomotives operating into California were required to use these shrouds to avoid detection by possible invading foreign aircraft. *Mike Schafer collection*

always particularly appreciative of the graphic side of Santa Fe's themes, from the Indian-headdress representation of its red-and-silver locomotives to the elegantly framed turquoise stone that decorated the private dining room of the *Super Chief*'s Pleasure Dome Lounge.

While growing up in Rockford, Illinois, in the early 1960s, I used to scan the Sunday *Chicago Tribune*'s travel section for rail-travel stories and passenger-train ads. If you didn't see a Santa Fe advertisement of some sort in the Sunday *Trib*, well, the railroad must've been on strike. Those Santa Fe ads inspired dreams of travel on a *Chief*.

Santa Fe heavily promoted its trains in local newspapers, with good results. Spot ads like this for the *Chief* and *San Francisco Chief* were aimed at Chicagoans. *Mike Schafer collection*

The theming of Santa Fe's passenger trains paid homage to Native Americans and invited passengers to see Western history right from their seats aboard a *Chief*. *Mike Schafer collection*

Finally, during the summer of 1965 came my long-awaited first trip on the Santa Fe. It wasn't particularly long—38 miles—but we did what we could on our meager resources in those days. A high-school buddy and I were heading for Joliet, one of the all-time great train-watching locations in the United States, and we opted for the Chicago–Los Angeles *Chief* to get us there from Chicago.

Once aboard the long, gleaming streamliner at Dearborn Station, we were awestruck by the stylish interiors. Carpeted floors in the coaches? Unheard of on the Illinois Central. Super comfortable coach seating with full leg rests and adjustable headrests? Never before in my lifetime. And piped-in soft music throughout the train too. The big attraction for us was the *Chief*'s exotic social center: the Big Dome Lounge—85 feet of lounge and seating area entirely under glass with a downstairs café area.

Since that first trip, I rode the *Chief* on several occasions, including one instance where, because of heavy holiday travel, the train was dispatched from Chicago in two sections. But my saddest trip on the *Chief* was its last on May 13, 1968. Like numerous other railroads of that period, Santa Fe had been shorn of its mail contracts by the U.S. Post Office, prompting the railroad to cut its own passenger system to a core network of trains—principally the *Super*

Chief, El Capitan, Texas Chief, San Francisco Chief, and the *Grand Canyon*. The *Chief* was not included, so in the wee hours of that May morning, three of us rode the final eastbound *Chief* across Illinois.

The Most Talked-About Train

During the early, frigid months of 1964—when the Rivieras were at No. 5 on the Top 40 chart with their hit single "(Warm) California Sun"—I happened across an ad in the Sunday *Chicago Tribune* inviting readers to write for information about "America's Most Talked-About Train," the *California Zephyr* (*CZ*). I did, and in return received a colorful brochure extolling the virtues of the Chicago-Oakland (San Francisco) Vista-Dome streamliner, jointly operated by the Burlington, Rio Grande, and Western Pacific railroads. I was hooked on the *CZ*.

Alas, the farthest our family ever traveled away from home (or could afford to travel) was Chicago, 85 miles away. California might as well have been a zillion miles away. My dream of traveling on the *CZ* across the prairies and through the Colorado Rockies and California's Feather River Canyon remained just that—a dream.

I finally saw the *California Zephyr* in the flesh (well, stainless steel) in 1965 and many times after that during numerous jaunts to Chicago, but my opportunities to ride it remained nonexistent. In spring 1968, the *CZ* became the subject of a college term paper for which I received an A+. My professor was so inspired by the paper that he and his family traveled to California on the *CZ* the following summer.

My chance finally came in 1969 during a marathon 10,000-mile-plus auto trip with two buddies to document Western railroading. We had

Santa Fe's westbound *Chief* treads its way out of Chicago in 1966 with an impressive train filled with summer travelers. The *Chief* offered what no other Chicago–West Coast streamliners could: a one-night-out schedule to California! Westbound the *Chief* left Chicago at 9 A.M. and arrived at Los Angeles just before midnight the following day—a tribute to Santa Fe's direct, high-speed main line between the two cities.

49

The under-dome lounge area of Santa Fe's Big Dome Lounge cars featured a Native American motif, with Indian sand paintings adorning glass dividers. The decor continued on wall murals and window curtains. *Bob Johnston*

photographed the *California Zephyr* at numerous locations in Colorado, Utah, and California, but a spur-of-the-moment change in our already convoluted itinerary actually put friend Richard Dean and me aboard the train at Oakland, California, for a 198-mile journey to Oroville, California. There, our third traveler, Jim Boyd, would rejoin us in the car.

For the grand, famous train that it was, the *California Zephyr*'s point of origination at Oakland was inauspicious, at best: a single track beside a paved platform at Western Pacific's freight yard. Known as the "launching pad," here is where passengers originating in downtown San Francisco were bused to board the train.

Once away from the launching pad, the *CZ* literally took to the streets of Oakland, traversing the double-track Western Pacific main line down Third Street to reach the stately Western Pacific depot. The *CZ*'s call here—and this was where we boarded—was a mini-event. As train time neared, railroad personnel erected barricades around the boarding area

Although the sight of a full-fledged passenger train invading a city street is, to say the least, unconventional, it did (and still does) happen in a few U.S. cities. For 22 years, the original *California Zephyr* trundled through the streets of Oakland, California, twice daily, stopping at the Western Pacific depot at Third and Washington to board or detrain passengers. This is the Chicago-bound *CZ* at Oakland in July 1969.

The CZ—An Eight-Year-Old's Delight

By Joseph M. Welsh

My father was a frugal man who liked to travel. Determined to take full advantage of the pass privileges he earned as a railroader, he pored over the *Official Guide of the Railways* each year selecting destinations to visit and which trains to ride there. In 1965, he picked Colorado and the *California Zephyr*. His timing was perfect.

It was a period of transition for the passenger train. The Burlington Route, which for years operated a wonderful fleet of trains, was but a few months away from hiring a new chief executive who would turn the passenger department on its ear by questioning the very reason why the company operated its marvelous fleet of *Zephyrs*.

None of that mattered to an eight-year-old boy about to board the most talked-about train in America. Loaded with dome cars and bisecting some of the most spectacular scenery in the country, the *California Zephyr* may well have been the greatest streamliner ever operated. From its schedule, arranged to travel through scenery by daylight, to its crew—friendly, attentive, and competent—the *Zephyr* was a marvel of execution. The train had everything: sleeping cars, comfortable coach seats, a splendid diner, a unique lounge car, and plenty of free seats under glass in five separate dome cars. For months I studied *CZ* advertising and could barely contain my anticipation.

On the appointed day, we arrived at Chicago from Philadelphia via the Pennsylvania Railroad's *General*. After a few hours visiting *Windy City* sights, it was back to the lofty concourse of Chicago Union Station for the 3:10 P.M. departure of the *Zephyr*. Boarding a long-distance train is always a thrill for travelers of any age, for it brings with it the anticipation of the journey ahead.

After settling into our seats on the lower level of our dome coach, we were visited by our Zephyrette who informed us that tonight, "Dinner would be courtesy of the Burlington." It helped that my father had connections in the railroad business.

We enjoyed dinner as the CZ crossed the Mississippi River and passed through rural Iowa. Then it was back to the dome to watch the evening fall. The hypnotic effect of signals turning to red as they rushed past our train in the dark was complemented by the

This is the locomotive crew's view of the *California Zephyr* winding through Gore Canyon along the Colorado River on Rio Grande's main line through the Rockies. This photo has special significance because it was aboard the locomotives of a Rio Grande freight in the Rockies that Cyrus Osborne, General manager of Electro-Motive Division of General Motors, said he wished passengers could have the same unobstructed view that locomotive crews had. He followed up with sketches for a special sight-seeing passenger car, and the rest is history. *Jim Bauman*

sound of clanging grade-crossing bells quickly being left behind in the night. Sleep came easily.

The next morning we were awake bright and early for breakfast in the diner and then claimed a ringside seat in the dome. Snaking into the Denver Union Station area our train passed through an automatic washer which, with a little human help, ensured that our dome windows were sparkling clean for the portion of the journey just ahead—the highlight of the ride.

After departing Denver in the competent hands of the Denver & Rio Grande Western Railroad, the *California Zephyr* began its climb up the Front Range of the Rockies. From the dome, our golden yellow Rio Grande locomotives were readily visible as they hoisted our stainless-steel train up the grade. Passing from broad daylight into pitch dark, the *CZ* popped through the first of 46 tunnels we would traverse that day and then entered Boulder Canyon. The morning passed quickly as a series of vignettes that remain etched in my mind: my father filming the trip with his 8-millimeter movie camera as craggy rocks seemed to loom dangerously close to our dome; the train diving into the 6.2-mile-long Moffat Tunnel; long-abandoned shacks near the rushing Colorado River (had they belonged to long-gone prospectors?).

My father, himself a former Rio Grande man, struck up a conversation with the grizzled old conductor in the vestibule of our car. Keeping an eye on his train as he talked, the veteran crewman poured tobacco and rolled a cigarette with one hand. Then Dad and I were off to lunch with Mom in the dome lounge's Cable Car Room. Soon it was time to gather our things as the train skimmed past the red rock walls of Glenwood Canyon. Our destination was Glenwood Springs, Colorado, for a few days of horseback riding, sightseeing, and lounging by the hot springs pool. For me, the highlights were the trips to the Glenwood Springs station to watch Denver & Rio Grande Western freights muscle their way through the canyon. Equal to that was the return trip on that most memorable of trains, the *CZ*, which made a lifelong lover of railroads out of this eight-year-old boy.

to keep wayward motorists from plunging into milling passengers. Then, a distant horn signaled No. 18's approach, and shortly the train eased to a halt in front of the depot.

Once entrained, we of course headed straight for one of the Vista-Dome coaches—after all, domes and scenery were what the *CZ* was all about. The late-morning departure meant we could enjoy lunch—a rather unremarkable chicken á la king—on the train as it worked its way through Fremont and Stockton.

A well-advertised feature of the original *CZ* was its train hostess, or "Zephyrette." Ours was Beulah Ecklund and although we had heard her announcements over the PA system, we had not yet seen her in person. After lunch I found Miss Ecklund at the Dutch door in one of the vestibules, enjoying the warm California sun while waiting to inspect No. 17, the westbound *CZ*, which we were about to meet at Phillips siding near Sacramento. I introduced myself and then we watched No. 17 coast by while our train stood in the siding. All *CZ* crews knew one another, and there was much waving between the two trains.

Beulah came back to our coach seats where she posed for photos. Naturally, the talk focused on her fascinating job followed by my obligatory, "Where do you hail from?"

"Oh," she said, half smiling, "a little town in northern Illinois you've never heard of." Miss Ecklund, of course, had no idea I was from Illinois.

"Try me," I politely challenged.

"Kirkland," she stated skeptically.

Following pages
My how the scenery has changed: The transition from city streets to the paradise that is California's Feather River Canyon happened in the space of about four hours. The 100-plus-mile Feather River Canyon, which provided Western Pacific with a low-grade entrance into California (the parallel Southern Pacific had to use the treacherous Donner Pass), was a fairly remote, unknown chasm until it was put on the map in 1949 by the new *California Zephyr*. Here, the eastbound *CZ* rides high above Spanish Fork in the canyon at Keddie, California.

Vista-Dome COACHES

Comfort and convenience are outstandingly apparent in the coaches.

Above: Dome cars were still a relatively new innovation when the *California Zephyr* was inaugurated in March 1949, so early *CZ* promotions included detailed cutaway views of dome cars to show potential travelers how such cars were cleverly engineered and how interiors were arranged. *Joe Welsh Collection* Right: The *CZ* gets serviced during the late-evening stop at Omaha, Nebraska. *Jim Heuer*

"*Kirkland?*" I exclaimed. "Why, I drive through there on my daily commute between Rockford and Northern Illinois University!"

Such was the improbable start of a continuing friendship that now includes her railroader-husband Jim Bauman. Beulah and I kept in touch from the start, and whenever she was on layover at the Chicago end of a *CZ* run, I would stop at Kirkland to visit her and her wonderful father.

I never did ride the original *CZ* cross-country, but I was at trackside for the train's widely publicized passing on March 22, 1970, photographing the final eastbound run leaving Galesburg, Illinois, for Chicago while in my mind the Rivieras' 1964 hit tune played over and over. Fortunately, this story has a happy ending. Amtrak resurrected the *California Zephyr* in 1983, albeit with all-new Superliner rolling stock and a partially revised routing. As part of the

A Zephyrette Remembers

By Beulah Bauman

Looking through my photos and thinking back to my involvement with the *California Zephyr* brought many names and faces back to mind. What a team effort it was to ensure that all our passengers enjoyed an experience of a lifetime on America's Most Talked-About Train!

Conductors such as Don Downer and Bob Chenowith—both the epitome of team captains—were a pleasure to work with, very diplomatic and gracious and yet firm when the situation called for it. Dining-car stewards and staff really made working on the train a wonderful experience. Many times there was coffee in a demitasse cup at the Zephyrette's door for a "wake-up" call to get us going for the day. CZ engineers like Bob "Rapid Robert" Coe and Herb Johnson were dedicated to keeping the train on time (or as close as possible). When he was off duty, Herb would often leave flowers at the Creston, Iowa, stop for Zephyrettes passing through.

There were other "guardian angels" who made our trips very pleasurable. "Pete the Italian" met

Five days before Christmas 1968, *Zephyr*ette Beulah Ecklund greets Santa Claus (a.k.a. John Bowling), who boarded the *California Zephyr* at Grand Junction, Colorado. Santa was a regular on the *CZ* during the holidays, greeting children and adult passengers alike. Extra touches like this made the *CZ* a family-oriented train quite unlike most others. *Beulah Bauman collection*

every CZ at Grand Junction and brought the Zephyrette a cup of coffee. Even people who simply lived along the CZ route would wave to the crews of each passing train and flash their porch light after dark as we passed by.

The people and supervisors who worked behind the scenes made the job the best one I've ever had. Our boss—or perhaps more correctly our "mother hen"—was Mary Lou Gordon who took an interest in each one of us both on the job and off. I can recall meeting Chicago Burlington & Quincy President Harry Murphy in the Vista-Dome lounge-observation car one afternoon shortly after I was hired. I did not know who he was until the trainman later informed me, but he was very kind and down to earth, and I never felt uncomfortable talking to him. One Western Pacific employee who stood out among the many who supported us and the CZ was Art Lloyd. I was additionally honored to rechristen Amtrak's *California Zephyr* with Art in 1983.

There was an incredible family feeling among our fellow railroaders. I would bake a cake for crew members who I knew would be making their last trip before retiring, and often I would bring home walnuts from California and share them with Milwaukee Road train crews who worked the *City* streamliners that I rode back to Davis Junction, Illinois, on my way home from a CZ trip.

Finally, there were the many *Zephyr*ettes with whom I shared a most unique transportation employment, among them Marie Krapf, Gale Consodine, Cathy Moran, Elizabeth Leibfort, Phyllis Olsta, and Linda Hein. Many of the girls lived in communities along the CZ route, while little Kirkland, Illinois (on the route of the *City* streamliners), had the distinction of being the home of two *Zephyr*ettes, Linda Hein and me.

Looking back, I feel that the *California Zephyr*'s appeal was that it reflected life's journey. There were different challenges to meet on every trip, and the scenery was constantly changing. There were a few detours and delays, but it was always high adventure, and our fellow crew members often made the difference between a pleasurable trip or one that was excruciating. The *California Zephyr* was an experience I will remember for the rest of my life.

The *CZ*'s Vista-Dome sleeper-lounge-observation car was for the exclusive use of first-class passengers. This view from the dome steps looks rearward. Drinks and other refreshments were dispensed from a small bar in an additional lounge area under the dome. The bedrooms were located in the forward half of the car. This was *the* car to be assigned to on the "World's Most Talked-About Train."

special first-run ceremony, Amtrak invited Beulah to don her Zephyrette uniform and ride the first westbound trip, greeting passengers and pointing out scenic highlights. And this she did, just as she had been doing some 13 years earlier.

Not until 1987 did I finally achieve my dream of riding the *CZ* all the way to California. Even under the Amtrak banner, it was a grand experience, one that brought back memories of the serendipitous events of that short ride to Oroville in 1969.

Chapter 5

STREAMLINER DINING

*I*n the heyday of streamliners, the railroads competed heavily among themselves as much as they did with other forms of transportation. Railroads lured travelers onto their streamliners with speed, scheduling, and exotic rolling stock. For example, advertisements for Santa Fe's new Pleasure Dome car on the *Super Chief* in 1951 undoubtedly wooed passengers away from Rock Island–Southern Pacific's *Golden State* on the Chicago–Kansas City–Los Angeles market.

Dining car service was one of those enticements. When all other considerations were equal, quality of

Dining aboard a passenger train remains one of the most pleasing experiences of rail travel. The reputation of some streamliner dining cars and their staffs put them on an equal with that of four-star restaurants—a claim that could be made by a number of railroads, including the Southern Railway, whose *Southern Crescent* dining service delighted hungry travelers until 1979. These passengers aboard the New Orleans–bound *Southern Crescent* in 1978 are about to experience homemade biscuits and other breakfast specialties.

Above: Gulf Mobile & Ohio dining service once rated mention in the *Chicago Tribune* in the early 1960s; the railroad offered quality food service right up to Amtrak takeover. Pride of the "Gee-Mo" fleet was the *Abraham Lincoln*, shown just prior to its departure from St. Louis Union Station for Chicago on a bright morning in the late 1950s. Facing page top: GM&O serving plates featured the company's memorable winged log. Facing page bottom: A dinner menu circa 1970 signed by longtime GM&O steward Jeff Powers featured a pen-and-ink rendering of *Abe Lincoln*'s home in Springfield, Illinois, on the route of the streamliner *Abraham Lincoln*. *Alvin Schultze*

dining-car food and service could mean the difference between choosing Lackawanna's *Phoebe Snow* or New York Central's *Empire State Express* on a trip from New York to Buffalo. Indeed, many railroads offered specialty dishes that became almost a trademark of that company, or at least one of its streamliners.

Dinner "Turns" on the *Abraham Lincoln*

Gulf Mobile & Ohio might have seemed an unlikely carrier for offering top-notch dining service. By the 1960s, the "Gee-Mo" was in the "also ran" league of railroads—companies overshadowed by

the likes of Great Northern, Santa Fe, and Seaboard Air Line—and its Chicago–St. Louis passenger trains had a certain down-home grittiness to them.

Gulf Mobile & Ohio's investments in newer passenger rolling stock had been minimal. In 1948, the railroad purchased 11 streamlined coaches and 4 parlor cars and in 1950 4 streamlined sleeping cars. That was it. So, when the railroad retired the last of its two 1937-era former-Baltimore & Ohio *Royal Blue* streamliner train sets from *Abraham Lincoln* service circa 1968, it had to provide food service using still serviceable 1920s-era heavyweight diner-lounges.

(a suit jacket with tails, for those of you who've never been out of a T-shirt).

My favorite entree was the "Fried Chicken, Half Disjointed, Country Style." Country style was a sort of diet-friendly way of saying "fried," and the "disjointed" nomenclature always prompted some humorous comments among us. The complete dinner cost $3.75 and led off with your choice of Fruit Cocktail–Maraschino, Soup Puree Split Pea, Chilled Tomato Juice or Consommè, Hot or Jellied. A head-lettuce salad followed shortly, and then the entree, with your choice of whipped potatoes, buttered lima beans, hashbrowns, or stewed tomatoes.

These battleships soon became a fixture on the otherwise all-streamlined *Abraham Lincoln*.

Not that it mattered. Gulf Mobile & Ohio dining car crews could prepare dinner (or breakfast or lunch) with the best of them, regardless of how elderly the kitchen and dining room were. And they did this well enough to earn a mention in the travel section of the Sunday *Chicago Tribune*!

Prompted by a friend of mine from Joliet, Illinois, whose father worked for the Gulf Mobile & Ohio railroad, several of us began a ritual that would last into the Amtrak era: "dinner turns" on the GM&O. We would take train 3, the southbound *Abe Lincoln*, out of Chicago at 5:05 P.M. (or out of Joliet at 5:50 P.M.) and ride as far as Bloomington, Illinois (arrival, 7:20 P.M.), thus allowing plenty of time for one of the railroad's sumptuous dinners. After a 12-minute layover at Bloomington, we would return home on northbound train 4, the *Limited*, at 7:32 P.M. No. 4 also carried a diner-lounge, and that's where we headed for dessert.

The regular steward on the *Abe* in the late 1960s and early 1970s was Mr. J. Powers, a distinguished-looking gentleman who wore black coattails

ABRAHAM LINCOLN'S HOME   SPRINGFIELD--ILLINOIS

Menu

Gulf, Mobile and Ohio Railroad

Other entrees on the Gulf Mobile & Ohio menu included a cheese omelet dinner, ocean perch, broiled pork chops, and broiled sirloin. A particularly popular item was the "GM&O Special Sandwich" ($2.25), a club affair with sliced chicken breast, Swiss cheese, bacon, lettuce, tomato, sliced hard-boiled egg, and Thousand Island dressing, all topped with a dollop of caviar.

The food was served on heavy-duty GM&O china, white rimmed in rose with the GM&O winged logo, and you ate your chicken using heavy silverware, also emblazoned with the GM&O herald. Today, a Gulf Mobile & Ohio dinner plate commands several hundred dollars at railroad antique shows. Times, they do change.

When Amtrak took over Gulf Mobile & Ohio's service in 1971, the old standard dining cars briefly remained in service, followed by Union Pacific diner-lounges. Mr. Powers still seated us. When Amtrak introduced its French-built Turboliners to Chicago–St. Louis service in 1973, however, full dining service became a casualty. Travelers were left with little more than prepackaged sandwiches dispensed cafeteria-style in the Turbo's dinette area. Progress, you know.

Pleasant Under Glass

So, what was the best train-dining experience? In later years, Santa Fe and Union Pacific were probably the top contenders of railroad dining. Twice I experienced Santa Fe's famous Champagne Dinner aboard the *Super Chief* and did so in the company of fine friends in the Turquoise Room. That private seven-person dining area, set off at one end of the Pleasure Dome Lounge car, offered a dining experience quite unlike others.

The award for my favorite rail dining experience must go to Union Pacific, however—specifically for a dinner aboard what I feel was the ultimate rolling restaurant, the dome diners that were a feature of the *City of Portland* and the *City of Los Angeles*. Union Pacific's move to add domes to its transcons was perhaps partly a case of one-upmanship. In 1949, Burlington, Rio Grande, and Western Pacific had inaugurated their immensely successful domeliner *California Zephyr*—the first transcontinental streamliner to carry domes. Then in 1950, Santa Fe took delivery of its Pleasure Dome Lounge cars, and in 1954, Northern Pacific, Burlington, and Spokane, Portland & Seattle introduced domes to their *North Coast Limited*. Meanwhile, Union Pacific transcons remained domeless.

Not that Union Pacific didn't have any dome experience. In 1950, the railroad had purchased the General Motors/Pullman-Standard experimental domeliner *Train of Tomorrow*, outshopped in 1947,

Many dining-car foods were prepared from scratch aboard the train. This Chicago, Burlington & Quincy chef pauses for a proud pose while preparing a pie for *Zephyr* passengers. *Bob Johnston*

Waiters aboard Great Northern's *Empire Builder* in 1968 sported smart uniforms trimmed in the road's signature colors: green and orange. Dining-car crews had to work out of an extremely confined kitchen/galley area that housed not only a remarkable array of foodstuffs but everything necessary to serve them—all types of crockery, pewterware, and silverware. *Bob Johnston*

and placed it in local Seattle-Portland service. The *Train of Tomorrow* featured a dome coach, dome diner, dome sleeper, and a dome lounge-observation car. Union Pacific must have gotten especially good feedback (pun intended) from Portland-Seattle passengers using the *Train of Tomorrow*'s dome diner. Union Pacific's impressive order for new equipment in the mid-1950s included 40 new dome cars from American Car & Foundry, 10 of which were dome diners.

These cars featured booth seating in the glass-enclosed dome as well as table seating (round tables, no less—a rarity in railroad dining cars) on part of the main level. The kitchen occupied the other portion of the main level. Taking a cue from Santa Fe's Turquoise

Text continued on page 68

This woman is about to enjoy the trademark treat of the *Super Chief*—the Champagne Dinner—as waiter Leo Fisher starts the feast with a glass of bubbly. *Bob Johnston*

Homeward Bound

By Deborah B. Goldfeder

I remember the morning when I knew without a doubt that I could never go home again. I heard the voice of a friend on the phone telling me that "my train" was "on the ground" in northern Virginia. My thoughts were for "my family" who were on the train that morning—people with whom I was never to ride again.

I had always known I was home when I boarded the Southern Railway, whether I was in Atlanta, Washington, New Orleans, or any intermediate stops. I long ago lost count of the time I spent on the *Southern Crescent*. I would walk into the diner and look at the brilliantly white linen-covered tables set with heavy silver-plate and china, and when I saw the yellow chrysanthemums and greenery in the bud vases I knew I was among family.

I never cared much for traveling or dining alone. Women in the early 1970s weren't often seen alone in diners. An alternative was to have your dinner brought to your sleeping-car room for an additional 50 cents, and coach passengers could go to the lounge car for more portable food to take back to

Southern Railway's handsome menu for the *Southern Crescent*, circa 1978. *Mike Schafer collection*

their seats. Those would have been my inclinations on every other railroad in the country except for the Southern. I averaged two round-trips a month between Atlanta and Washington, D.C., from 1973 to 1977. My pass (I was married to a Southern employee) got me half a roomette plus full transportation, so travel was very inexpensive. I usually had to pay only for part of my roomette and my dining car meals. And what meals they were!

Bread and Butter Pudding; Vanilla Sauce

Grease sides and bottom of pudding pan, then dice bread placing layer on bottom of pan, sprinkle with sugar and butter and a little cinnamon between each layer of bread until pan is full.

Beat 2 eggs with 3 cups of milk with a little salt. Pour this over bread, let stand one hour then bake slowly for 3/4 hour, then uncover and brown.

Serve in fruit saucer underlined with doily and tea plate. Spoonfull [sic] of vanilla sauce on top. A la carte, serve in oatmeal bowl.

Vanilla sauce: Use prepared vanilla pudding mixture, cutting the pudding to the proper consistency for a sauce.

The steward usually seated me in Mr. Coleman's section and gave me the form to write down my order, but that was never really necessary to get what I wanted. Although waiters were not permitted to take verbal orders on trains then, Mr. Coleman would ask if I wanted my usual meal and then bring it to me with no further instructions. I ordered the same thing every time: tomato juice, prime rib of beef natural (medium rare), flaked potatoes, green beans, combination salad with blue cheese dressing on the side, half grapefruit substituted for the usual desserts, and iced tea with lemon, all for $7.15 in 1977.

Regular Southern patrons would say it was heresy to substitute anything for the bread-and-butter pudding with vanilla sauce, especially if Mr. Price was the chef. I always stopped by the kitchen to compliment the dining car staff after dinner, and one day I asked Mr. Price to share his secret for his particularly delicious bread pudding. Dining-car recipe books rarely gave exact measurements, so each chef was free to add his own special touches. It seems that Mr.

Price had been audited by the railroad for excessive use of eggs. An internal auditor I knew well rode with Mr. Price several times to determine why he used 25 percent more eggs than did other chefs. All the auditor really needed to do was to ask what was different about his bread-and-butter pudding. Mr. Price used an extra egg with each batch he made. He warned me to watch out for that auditor because, "... he will short you on them eggs now!"

According to the official service book for dining car crews at the time, the recipe is shown above.

On those many occasions when I traveled on the Southern, the one thing I could count on was the hospitality and service in the dining car. "My" crew was on the *Southern Crescent* when it derailed in Alma, Virginia, on December 3, 1978. They were preparing breakfast for another group of passengers who would have been made to feel they were special to the crew when the special people were the dining-car staff themselves. In a few short weeks, Amtrak took over the *Crescent,* but it was never the same. More than 20 years later, I still miss them.

Room innovation, the dome diners each included a private 10-seat dining room, under the dome.

One of the nice things about the Union Pacific Domeliners that operated out of Chicago was that passengers could ride locally, more or less. So even if you weren't headed cross-country, one could still sample dome dining. And a number of us often did this in the late 1960s and in 1970, riding from Chicago to Davis Junction or Savanna, Illinois, for a domed dinner.

My "usual" on Union Pacific diners was the Special Sirloin Steak Dinner for about $5.50—a considerable sum in 1970, but always well worth the guilt that ensued for such decadent spending while trying to put myself through college. The soup course, including garlic-flavored toasted French rolls, was usually on the table by the time the *City* eased out of the north sheds of Union Station. To be "floating" among the skyscrapers of Chicago in a glass-roofed restaurant was an unforgettable experience.

The ultimate railway dining experience aboard a regularly scheduled passenger train just might have been Union Pacific's dome diners. Dinner patrons are just beginning to be seated in the dome dining section of the *City of Denver/City of Portland* as it eases out of Denver in 1967 for its overnight trip to Chicago. *Alvin Schultze*

Members of the North Western Illinois Chapter of the National Railway Historical Society congregate in the dome diner of the westbound combined *City* streamliners about to depart Chicago Union Station in the spring of 1970. To "float" high above the rails in a glass-roof dining room provided a culinary experience quite unlike others. *Jim Boyd*

The salad course—a quarter portion of head lettuce—soon followed. As the Domeliner neared its suburban Elgin stop, the "Charcoal Broiled Steak, Maitre d'Hotel," had been set before me. (Other entree choices included Broiled Brook Trout, Fried Disjointed Spring Chicken, and Roast Top Round of Beef.) After I turned 21 in 1970, this was always accompanied by California red wine ($1.25), bottled expressly for Union Pacific. By the time I cut into the steak, our train was clipping along at its 79-mile-per-hour maximum speed, and watching the semaphore signal arms drop as the train passed them was a bonus to the setting sun as it cast a warm glow over the Illinois cornfields. In the middle of those cornfields was the Davis Junction stop, 80 miles out of Chicago, by which time we had completed the desert course: Oregon Wild Berry Sundae being the obligatory choice, and, of course, coffee.

Inexplicably, Union Pacific pulled the dome diners from service several months prior to Amtrak's

The dining-car experience wasn't just for adults, of course. New York Central and other railroads used special menus to cater to younger folks. *C. W. Newton collection*

startup, replacing them with single-level streamlined diners. On the evening of April 1, 1971, several of us rode the last and final westbound Domeliner out of Chicago for one last dinner trip. The dome diners were gone, and although the food was just as splendid as ever, the effect wasn't quite the same. It just wasn't as magical as it had been, under glass.

Chapter 6

SOUTHERN STREAMLINERS

Warm Memories

rom the Carolinas into Texas, America's South has been a popular travel destination for decades. The lure of Florida palms, gulf breezes, and year-round hospitable climes played heavy into the creation of some of the greatest streamliners. Paramount among these were the Northeast-to-Florida fleet: Atlantic Coast Line's *Champion*s and *Florida Special* and Seaboard Air Line's *Silver Meteor* and *Silver Star*.

Likewise, the sweep of trains that carried passengers between the Northeast and mid-South destinations included other well-known streamliners: the *Southerner* and the *Crescent* (New York–Atlanta–New

Illinois Central's *Panama Limited* was unquestionably the finest train between the Midwest and the Gulf of Mexico. Commemorating the construction of the Panama Canal, the *Panama* was born in 1911 and streamlined in 1942. The southbound train is in the boarding process at Central Station, Chicago, in 1962; sleeper-lounge observation car *Memphis* is already being occupied by passengers wanting before-dinner drinks. Unfortunately this beautiful car was wrecked in 1965. *Alvin Schultze*

Orleans) and the *Tennessean* (Washington-*Memphis*).

And Midwest-to-the-South streamliners abounded: the *South Wind* and *Dixie Flagler* (Chicago-Florida); the *Southern Belle* (Kansas *City*–New Orleans), the *Humming Bird* and *City of New Orleans* (Chicago/St. Louis–New Orleans), the *Texas Special* and *Texas Eagle* (St. Louis–Texas points), and more.

Pullman ride on the *Humming Bird*

I had my first (and, as it would turn out, only) ride on a Pullman-operated sleeping car on a Southland streamliner. Following a four-day road trip to Alabama right after Christmas 1967, my friend John and I had to return to Illinois for work obligations while our buddy Jim continued on to Georgia. John

and I decided to "fly" home from Birmingham, Alabama, on Louisville & Nashville's *Humming Bird*. Jim deposited us at the modern little L&N depot in downtown Birmingham in early evening, and we bought two coach tickets to Chicago.

The *Humming Bird* was due in from New Orleans at 6:10 P.M. but was expected to be some 45 minutes late. We had spent the last two rainy days crammed into Jim's 1966 Volkswagen Beetle, so we were antsy for the comfort of a wide-open reclining-seat coach. Finally, we could hear the *Bird* thunder in overhead on the elevated station tracks. Crowds pressed toward the boarding gates.

Streamliner or not, this was the holiday season and Louisville & Nashville had pressed extra cars into

Railroads enticed travelers aboard their trains with elaborate folders and train brochures, and some of the most colorful promotions were for trains of the South. This Seaboard Air Line folder captured attention by featuring the railroad's new diesels with their flashy "citrus" paint scheme of deep green, yellow, and orange with black-and-silver trim. The opposing train in this idealized scene shows the all-stainless-steel *Silver Meteor*. Joe Welsh collection

THE SOUTHERNER

Streamliner
NEW YORK ... NEW ORLEANS
via ATLANTA and BIRMINGHAM

SOUTHERN

The Southerner

SR
THE SOUTHERN SERVES THE SOUTH

SOUTHERN RAILWAY SYSTEM

High on the list of several Southern Railway trains linking North and South was the New York–New Orleans *Southerner*, inaugurated in 1941. Silver ink was used on this *Southerner* folder to emphasize the train's new stainless-steel cars. The *Southerner* quickly became the railway's premier train, lasting until 1970 when its companion train, the *Crescent*, was discontinued and its name applied to the *Southerner's* restructured New York–Atlanta–New Orleans service: the *Southern Crescent*. Joe Welsh collection

service—modernized heavyweight equipment from the 1920s. We were directed to one of these dimly lit heavyweight coaches, packed with squealing children and transient old curmudgeons with hacking coughs. Once our tickets were lifted, we made haste for the diner-lounge, another older car modernized in the late 1940s by the railroad, yet retaining much of its original elegance. Despite the teeming masses aboard the train, the dining area was not crowded, and the attentive crew served up two superb fried chicken dinners.

Once back in our now overheated, rolling tenement of a coach, reality set in that it was going to be a long night. "John, whaddya say we get bedroom space?" Neither of us were exactly flush with cash, but facing a night of squalor loosened the purse strings. We commandeered the L&N conductor who

in turn took us to the Pullman conductor; yes, there was an unclaimed room.

Our new accommodation was a double bedroom in *Loblolly Pine*, a six-section, six-roomette, four-double bedroom sleeper built for the Chicago & Eastern Illinois in 1953. The beds—arranged parallel to the rails—had already been made down. For both of us, this was our first time aboard a sleeper, and we were in awe of the quiet, inviting surroundings. We marveled at the crisp, white linens, the neatly folded Pullman blankets, and the cleverly compact arrangement of such things as reading lights, clothes closet, wash sink, and private restroom facilities. It was $150 (first-class fare upgrade plus room charge) well spent.

John lost the coin toss and got the upper bunk. Soon it was lights out, but I propped myself up in bed

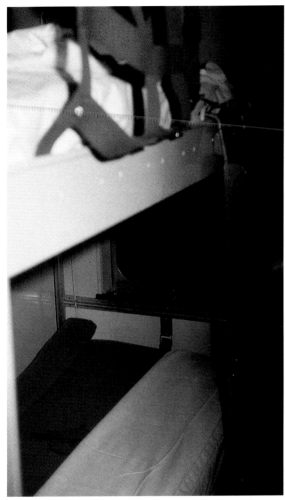

and watched the dark Tennessee countryside skim by the window as the *Humming Bird* raced up the L&N main line. I heard John overhead: "Boy, *this* is comfort!" Around midnight, the *Bird* entered Nashville Union Station.

The hour-long stop here was less conducive to sleep. At Nashville, the *Humming Bird* was split into a Chicago/St. Louis section and a Cincinnati section

Bedrooms, compartment, drawing rooms, and roomettes offered privacy that added a whole new dimension to rail travel. Any concern travelers might have had of the sometimes hefty extra costs of first-class rail fare—plus an accommodation charge—usually dissipated when they stretched out in comfy beds with fresh linens and thick Pullman blankets. This double bedroom, shown with the beds "made down," is typical of those that once carried thousands of slumbering passengers each night throughout America. *Charles Laird Sr., collection of David P. Oroszi*

Always an impressively long train in and out of Chicago, the combined *Humming Bird/Georgian* smokes out of Dearborn Station on a steamy July afternoon in 1966. Though technically a Chicago & Eastern Illinois train between Chicago and Evansville, Indiana, Louisville & Nashville diesels often worked through to Chicago while C&EI locomotives could be found on the L&N side of the operations.

and at the same time combined with the *Georgian* from Atlanta—a process that required a massive shuffling of cars. At the predawn stop at Evansville, Indiana, the St. Louis section was split from our Chicago section, and the latter would enter the Chicago & Eastern Illinois Railroad.

I awoke at dawn as our train pulled out of Terre Haute, Indiana, and crossed into the frosty state of Illinois, more than two hours behind schedule. Time for breakfast! Unlike the night before, the diner—a streamlined car that had originated in Atlanta on the *Georgian*—was bustling. We were seated with two sailors en route back to Great Lakes Naval Station at North Chicago and enjoyed good conversation over bacon and eggs and plenty of steaming coffee. Because of frigid outside temperatures, the car was

running a bit cold, and frost was beginning to cover the windows.

We had often seen and photographed the *Humming Bird/Georgian* during photo expeditions to Chicago and knew it to be a notoriously late time-keeper. Today was no exception, and we rolled to a stop at Dearborn Station some three hours later than the advertised 10:35 A.M. arrival.

By next spring, the Chicago sections of the *Humming Bird* and *Georgian* had been axed. We had made a wise choice in returning home on the *Humming Bird*.

Plane to the Train: the *Silver Meteor*

Introduced in 1939, Seaboard Air Line's *Silver Meteor* sparked the streamlining movement on the Northeast-to-Florida corridor and was an overnight sensation. Sixty years later, the *Silver Meteor*—now under the Amtrak banner and featuring all-new equip-ment—still leaves New York and Miami daily for its overnight journeys between the North and South.

I first saw the *Meteor* close-up while attending a convention in Miami Beach in 1965. I had always been intrigued by the Seaboard Air Line in general and its *Silver Meteor* in particular, so I snuck away

Pennsylvania Railroad's *South Wind* was one of a triumvirate of Chicago-Florida streamliners introduced prior to World War II, alternating departures from Miami and Chicago with Illinois Central's *City of Miami* and Chicago & Eastern Illinois-Louisville & Nashville's *Dixie Flagler*. Atlantic Coast Line diesels handle this day's southbound *South Wind* on the Pennsylvania Railroad at Logansport, Indiana, on November 16, 1952. The *Wind* became the only Midwest-Florida train to survive into Amtrak. *Sandy Goodrick*

from convention activities to Seaboard's shabby Miami station to witness the *Meteor* arrive from New York. Six years later, in 1971, I rode that train.

My former boss, Larry Carlson, had moved his family to a new life in Melbourne, Florida, and I visited them in the summer of 1971, traveling south to Orlando on the sole survivor of a once-impressive array of Midwest-Florida liners, the *South Wind*. My visit included witnessing a predawn satellite launch from Cape Kennedy. Later that same day, I was off to catch a railbound celestial celebrity. I had reservations on the *Meteor* out of Winter Haven, Florida, to Newark, New Jersey, and Larry promised to chauffeur me to Winter Haven.

Close friend that he was, Larry had (and as far as I know, still has) an annoying ability to completely lose track of time, and despite the urgings of his wife, Mary, and me, we left Melbourne way behind schedule. Along about Kissimmee, Florida, it became alarmingly clear that I would miss the *Meteor*'s 12:42 P.M. call at Winter Haven.

"Head to the Orlando airport!" I said, and we did. The travel gods were with me—National Airlines

The author's first look at Seaboard Air Line's *Silver Meteor* was at its cramped stub-end depot at Miami, Florida, where the *Meteor* is shown having just arrived from New York on an August afternoon in 1965. Launched in 1939, the *Meteor* was the first New York–Florida streamliner. The tavern-observation car in this scene was built by the Budd Company in 1947 for upgraded *Meteor* service. The car provided a congenial gathering point (below) for coach passengers. *Interior photo, Bob Johnston*

A *Silver Meteor* service cocktail napkin. *Oliver D. Joseph collection*

in disbelief and pointed the way to my room.

The *Cardinal* was a 1953 Budd product featuring 16 duplex roomettes and 4 double bedrooms. It and 10 sister cars were built for Baltimore & Ohio's *Capitol Limited* and *National Limited*, but when the cars became surplus, Baltimore & Ohio leased them to SCL, which marketed them as economy sleepers requiring only a modest charge above coach fare.

As the *Meteor* sped north from Jacksonville along SCL's former Seaboard Air Line route into Georgia, I headed for the end-of-train lounge observation car for a drink and sat watching the Georgia countryside recede behind the train. My only disappointment with the *Meteor* was the absence of its signature car, the glass-roofed Sun Lounge-sleeper, which on this trip was substituted with a more mundane former Atlantic Coast Line sleeper-lounge. The lounge area was nearly empty, save for passenger service representative R. Paul Carey, on hand to represent the new, fledgling Amtrak and assist passengers with travel-related problems. We talked at length about passenger trains and the unknown future of a three-month-old Amtrak.

Dinner as the sun disappeared behind blurring Georgia pine trees was perhaps the high point of this entirely pleasant trip. I was seated with a wonderfully spirited retired black woman who regaled me with anecdotes about life in Manhattan. Meanwhile, the dining car crew served up a stellar charcoal broiled sirloin steak with mushroom caps. After dinner we relocated to the lounge for more good conversation, both of us taking note of an eccentric New Yorker who was traveling with a rather large Doberman—in his roomette! At the Columbia, South Carolina, stop we saw him walking his dog while talking to no one in particular.

Slumber that night came easy, as the Seaboard main line provided a glass-smooth steel pathway through the Carolinas. I woke up briefly to see Raleigh, North Carolina, about 12:30 A.M. and slept right through the 3:30 A.M. stop at Richmond, Virginia, and our change to Richmond, Fredericksburg

had a flight already boarding for Jacksonville and New York. Not that I needed to, but I explained to the National agent that I missed my train to New York and had to get to Jacksonville to catch up to it. "But our flight ends up in New York," she offered.

I replied, "But does your plane have a private room with a full bed, a glass-roofed lounge area, and will a steak dinner be served . . . on real china?"

Jacksonville plane ticket in hand, I waved to the Carlsons and boarded the National DC9. Less than an hour later I was in Jacksonville, somewhere in those 150 air-miles having overtaken the *Meteor*. A taxi ride from the airport put me at cavernous Jacksonville Union Station more than an hour ahead of the *Meteor*'s 4 P.M. arrival.

True to Seaboard Coast Line (the new name of the railroad after the Atlantic Coast Line/Seaboard Air Line merger in 1967) form, the *Meteor* rolled in (backed in, actually) on time, and I presented myself to the car attendant standing outside the sleeper *Cardinal* serving as the train's "Budget Room Coach." The surprised attendant had given me up as a no-show, but I explained my plight—or flight, as it were. He laughed

A close-up view of one corner of Seaboard's Sun Lounge sleepers reveals a radio—and a fake mural depicting a coastal Florida scene. Despite what train brochures may have shown, it was virtually impossible to catch glimpses of the Atlantic Ocean from a Seaboard train. Seaboard Air Line followed a relatively unscenic inland routing between Jacksonville and West Palm Beach, Florida. *Bob Johnston*

& Potomac diesels. Further, I snoozed right through the 20-minute dawn stop at Washington, D.C., where we exchanged the Richmond, Fredericksburg & Potomac diesels for a pair of powerful Penn Central GG1 electric locomotives. When daylight finally goaded me into consciousness, the *Meteor* was cruising at 90 miles per hour up Penn Central's four-track electrified Northeast Corridor main line.

Seeing my prior night's dinner companion already seated in the diner for breakfast, I joined her for still more great conversation and a fine ham-and-eggs breakfast that included grits. On time at 10 A.M., the *Meteor* rushed to a stop at Newark Pennsylvania Station where I got off the train to meet waiting friends. That first trip on the *Meteor* remains one of my favorite.

Chapter 7

REGIONAL STREAMLINERS

Colorful Recalls

Regional streamliners—trains with runs of less than 500 miles—were a colorful lot. Not only did they outnumber the long-distance streamliners, but they came in all shapes, sizes, and colors. In fact, the first two true streamliners—Union Pacific's M-10000 and Burlington's *Zephyr* 9900—spent their entire careers in regional service.

The *Super Chief* may have gotten you from Chicago to Los Angeles, but if you were continuing on to, say, Santa Barbara, a regional streamliner

Southern Pacific was a California institution dating from the late 1800s. In the mid-1900s "Espee" operated an impressive array of regional streamliners, led by its most-famous train ever, the *Coast Daylight*, linking California's two largest metropolitan areas, Los Angeles and San Francisco. Introduced in 1937, the red-and-orange *Daylight* was often called "The Most Beautiful Train in the World," and it traversed some of California's best scenery. In this view from aboard the northbound *Coast Daylight* in the late 1950s, the train negotiates Cuesta Pass in the Santa Margarita Range above San Luis Obispo. *Alvin Schultze*

81

Go Great...Go Streamlined

Internationals

Between

SEATTLE • VANCOUVER
Washington   British Columbia

GREAT NORTHERN RAILWAY

504

504

THE INTERNATIONAL

Although the Great Northern Railway is most closely associated with its "Incomparable *Empire Builder*," GN's streamlined *International* between Seattle, Washington, and Vancouver, British Columbia, offered luxury regional service between the United States and Canada. *Joe Welsh collection*

would complete the journey—Southern Pacific's *Coast Daylight* in this case. Heading from St. Paul, Minnesota, to Vancouver, British Columbia? Most of your trip might have been on Great Northern's incomparable *Empire Builder*, but the last 156 miles—Seattle to Vancouver—would have been aboard Great Northern's streamlined *International*. And, of course, one could use a regional streamliner within its own domain. Residents of Indianapolis, Indiana, for example, might have relied on New York Central System's *James Whitcomb Riley* for trips to Lafayette, Indiana; Cincinnati, Ohio; or Chicago.

I grew up with a regional streamliner (chapter 2), and most of my streamliner sojourns were aboard regional runs, but my memories of them were just as indelible as those of the "big guy" streamliners.

New York, New York, on the New Haven Railroad

While on a week-long photography expedition in the Northeast by car in the spring of 1968, my cohorts, Jim and Bill, and I decided to make a side trip into America's largest metropolis. I had never seen New York City, so this was an event that called for more than a mundane drive through the Holland Tunnels into the morass of Manhattan. We wanted to arrive there in style—and we did, on New York, New Haven & Hartford's crack *Merchants Limited*.

We boarded at New Haven, Connecticut, where the premier streamliner of the 230-mile Boston–New York route eased in from Boston at 7:45 P.M. New Haven was the east end of the railroad's electrified district out of New York City, so many trains changed between diesel and electric locomotives here. Our *Merchants* had dual-mode diesel-electric/electric locomotives this evening, so no engine change was necessary, and at 7:53 P.M. we were off and running.

The New Haven Railroad of this era was synonymous with financial turmoil, and even on the *Merchants* this was apparent. The fluted stainless-steel cars dating from 1949 bore battle scars and worn seat fabrics. Regardless, a sense of expeditiousness

THE
James Whitcomb Riley

DE-LUXE ALL COACH STREAMLINER

CINCINNATI • INDIANAPOLIS • LAFAYETTE • KANKAKEE • CHICAGO

NEW YORK CENTRAL SYSTEM

The brochure announcing the newly streamlined *Riley* featured an artist's rendering of one of the railroad's two Pacific-type (4-6-2) steam locomotives that received streamlined shrouding for *Mercury* and *Riley* service. For obvious reasons, they were referred to as "upside-down bathtubs," and the shrouding was removed by the end of the 1940s. *Joe Welsh collection*

Named for Indiana's most-famous poet, the *James Whitcomb Riley* was the star regional train of the Cleveland, Cincinnati, Chicago & St. Louis Railroad—the Big Four Route—a subsidiary of the New York Central. Streamlined in 1941, the Cincinnati-Chicago speedster in 1971 acquired the dubious distinction of being the only New York Central train name to survive the Penn Central merger—in part due to the efforts of the *Riley* Booster Club, which heavily promoted the train. The *Riley* is shown having just arrived at Chicago's Central Station in 1970 with an observation car chartered by the club. *Jim Heuer*

prevailed as our train sped smoothly westward beside Long Island Sound under a canopy of catenary wire supported by a marvelous array of girder work, the very same girder work that inspired toy magnate Alfred Carlton Gilbert to create his famous Erector toy construction set in 1911. This had double meaning for me, as I grew up on American Flyer trains and Erector Sets, both products of New Haven–based A. C. Gilbert Company.

We slipped into the dining car, *Miles Standish*, for the last call to dinner. We perused the *Merchants'*

menu while watching the urban sprawl rush past our wide window in June twilight. It was obvious that New Yorkers cherished their spirits, for the menu devoted a whole page to a wine and liquor list surrounded by ads for Gordon's gin and Haig blended Scotch whiskey—"Haig is Happening on the New Haven," one ad shouted in all capital letters.

I was not old enough to legally toast my first look at New York City with Great Western Champagne ($2.00 for an 8-ounce bottle), but the meal had a celebratory air about it anyway. The cheapskate in me

New Haven's *Merchants Limited* (left in photo) shares the subterranean platforms of New York's Grand Central Terminal with a Penn Central suburban train shortly after arrival from Boston in 1969. The diner is partially visible at left followed by two parlor cars. New Haven's colorful orange-and-black livery on shiny stainless-steel sheathed cars hid the ominous fact that the legendary old carrier was bankrupt.

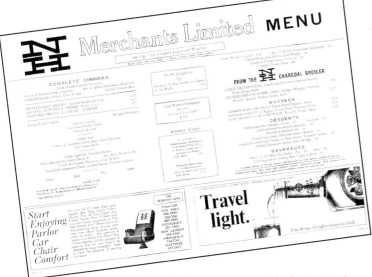

New Haven's menus were unique in that they incorporated outside advertising, generating badly needed revenue for the dining-car department—traditionally a money-losing sector even during the best days of the streamliners.

settled for the New Haven Club Sandwich ($2.95), but Jim went all out with a sirloin steak dinner ($5.50). Bill opted for Broiled Boston Scrod ($3.25).

At 9:15 P.M. the *Merchants* rolled to a stop in Grand Central. Laden with photography gear, we shambled along toward the waiting room. A quick self-guided tour of the landmark terminal led us back to the commuter platforms to catch the 10:05 P.M. New Haven local back to Connecticut.

I was totally fascinated by the passenger-oriented New Haven, but the railroad didn't make it into the 1970s; however, there's comfort in knowing that, 30 years later, the *Merchants Limited* still plies the old New Haven Shore Line Route.

North Woods by North Western

In 1957 and 1958, the Wisconsin Public Utilities Commission made a deal with the C&NW: The railway could discontinue some uneconomical secondary passenger trains within the state if in turn it would

Green Bay greeting: Northbound and southbound *Flambeau* *"400"*s meet at the Green Bay, Wisconsin, depot in August 1966. The author was traveling on the northbound train (left in distance), whose baggage-mail-tavern car, lead coach, and diner have been transferred to the rear end of the southbound at right. North of Green Bay, the *Flambeaus* were leisurely country locals; south of Green Bay they were high-speed corridor trains.

Enjoy the Greatest Travel Thrill Yet!

RIDE AMERICA'S FIRST BI-LEVEL STREAMLINERS

Get acquainted with an entirely new concept of travel comfort as you ride one of North Western's new Bi-Level "400" streamliners—America's most modern passenger trains. The ingenious design and engineering of these new trains sets a new pace in passenger car construction. Even the locomotive units have been re-designed so that they now furnish the power needed to provide all-electric heating, air conditioning and lighting for the entire train.

You'll like the full roominess of the seats and the whisper-quiet air cushioned ride. Take your scenery from the high or low level as you glide along in your comfort-engineered coach or parlor car seat. Enjoy freshly prepared meals in the spacious diner and refreshing beverages in the colorful new bi-level lounge. In fact, treat yourself to an entirely new travel thrill—ride the Bi-Level "400's" between Chicago, Green Bay and Upper Michigan.

TRAVEL COMFORT DESIGNED WITH YOU IN MIND

MORE INDIVIDUAL SEAT SPACE PER PASSENGER

Coach seats on both levels are "comfort-engineered" for easy riding and provide greater space than conventional seats. Single as well as double seating is provided.

PARLOR CARS WITH UPPER AND LOWER "SEE-LEVELS"

Elegant spaciousness keynotes the parlor car with its individual all-position easy chairs. Here you can enjoy the passing scene in quiet comfort from either level.

TWO-LEVEL LUXURY LOUNGE SERVICE

Toast your fellow travelers in the country club atmosphere of the bi-level Bar-Lounge. Built-in fixtures in the arm of each chair provide a self sufficient serving place for single seats. Table accommodations are available for groups of two or four.

SPACIOUS, SPARKLING DINING CARS

A planned effect of openness and colorful room decor makes dining on these trains a festive event. Here a varied menu of freshly prepared meals coupled with courteous service may be enjoyed as your train moves swiftly to its destination.

When the new bilevel equipment was introduced in 1958, Chicago & North Western issued a folder highlighting the unusual new cars. The statement that these were "America's First Bi-Level Streamliners" was only partially true, as Santa Fe's Hi-Level equipment—introduced in 1956—was certainly of bilevel design. Nonetheless, North Western's "gallery"-format bilevels, introduced on Chicago suburban trains in 1950, were new to intercity streamliners in 1958.

upgrade selected primary trains. Thus, the Chicago & North Western became the last railroad before Amtrak to re-equip a streamliner with new rolling stock.

North Western took an innovative approach by purchasing efficient all-electric "gallery"-type bilevel cars from Pullman-Standard.

North Western purchased ten coaches, one coach-lounge, one coach-parlor car, and one full parlor car, all bilevel. These cars were augmented by older single-level baggage-mail-tavern and dining cars rebuilt with false, high roofs to match, from an exterior viewpoint, the new bilevel equipment. The new and rebuilt cars went to work on the Chicago–Ishpeming (Michigan) *Peninsula "400,"* the Chicago–Green Bay *Green Bay "400,"* and the Chicago–Ashland (Wisconsin) *Flambeau "400."*

Text continued on page 90

The Chicago-bound *Flambeau "400"* calls at Ironwood, Michigan, during the 1970–1971 holiday season. When that holiday travel season ended a few days later, the train was replaced with a bus between Green Bay and Ashland, Wisconsin, and all Chicago & North Western intercity passenger trains were discontinued on April 30, 1971, leaving the once-bustling Chicago–Green Bay corridor high and dry.

Nothing Could Be Finer . . .

By Richard Kunz

. . . than to ride the *ElectroLiner* in the morning (or any other time, for that matter). The twin electric interurban streamliners that held down the premier Chicago North Shore & Milwaukee (North Shore Line) schedules between Chicago and Milwaukee for 22 years spawned a great many memories for this inveterate traveler.

In the earlier years, living in the Windy City with relatives 85 miles to the north meant regular trips to the Beer City on weekends and special occasions. Teenage independence and a genetic wanderlust resulted in much pleasure travel between the two metro areas. Whenever possible, right down to the last trip on that bitterly cold January night in 1963, the 'Liner was the train of choice.

The twin trains, built by St. Louis Car Company in 1941, ran on an easily remembered schedule—departures from either Chicago or Milwaukee at 8 A.M., 11 A.M., 2 P.M., 5 P.M., and 8 P.M., seven days a week, making the 88-mile trip in about two hours. That timing averages out to about 45 miles per hour for the entire trip, including several scheduled station stops and the torturous negotiation of Milwaukee streets and Chicago's 'L.'

For 22 years, two *ElectroLiner* streamliners of interurban Chicago North Shore & Milwaukee sprinted back and forth between Chicago and Milwaukee. Although the CNS&M was abandoned in January 1963, both of its Liners survived, going to work in Philadelphia suburban service as *Liberty Liners*. After their retirement early in the 1980s, both trains went to museums, with one having been restored to nearly original condition at its new home at the Illinois Railway Museum.

The tavern-lounge of the last northbound North Shore *ElectroLiner* is packed with farewell travelers on January 20, 1963. Writer Richard Kunz, then a North Shore employee, is seated at far left (with glasses). The man across the table, his face partially obscured by the woman in the foreground, is the late Tom Kopriva who that evening had the honor of being served the last "Electroburger" grilled on an *ElectroLiner*. Bob Johnston

Happily, food service was also available on the 10 *ElectroLiner* trips each day, in the gaily decorated, dancing-elephant-motif tavern-lounge car midship. It was a limited menu, to be sure (the "ElectroBurger" grilled to order was the house specialty), but dining on the 'Liner was a treat to be savored whenever the opportunity presented itself.

It was best to board the *ElectroLiners* at North Shore's Roosevelt Road terminal on the 'L.' There, at the train's point of origin, you stood a pretty good chance of getting the coveted front window seat just across from the motorman's cab.

And what a view you got from that exalted position: gliding importantly through the Loop gathering the fortunate few at Loop station stops amid wistful looks at the sleek salmon, green, and silver streamliner from riders relegated to mere 'L' trains of the Chicago Transit Authority.

The snaking around the myriad curves of the long structure leading to Howard Street through neighborhoods posh and plain. A last call at that major junction, and a dive into the tree-lined cut of the old Niles Center branch. Perhaps a stop at Dempster, the last outpost of urban civilization, followed by a dash along the magnificent Skokie Valley Route toward Waukegan.

After reporting at Waukegan's Edison Court station in that somnolent City, the cross-country view increasingly betrayed North Shore's true interurban heritage, with brief halts at the distinctive Kenosha and utilitarian Racine, Wisconsin, stations punctuating speedy spurts across the prairies.

A quick transit of the long embankment on the Beer City's south side led into a streetcar-like grind through the streets to the simple brick terminal at Sixth and Michigan. A unique Midwestern vista, as seen from the "catBird seat" of the *ElectroLiner*—and one hell of a ride!

In the mid-1960s, our family vacationed in northern Wisconsin. We always drove to Sugar Camp Lake near Rhinelander, but work obligations kept me home until later in the week when I would finally catch up with everyone—by riding the *Flambeau "400"* to Rhinelander. The *Flambeau* was an interesting train with a split personality.

My first *Flambeau* trip, in 1966, began at North Western Terminal in Chicago. As soon as the *Flambeau's* boarding announcement echoed through the vast waiting room of the terminal, crowds descended like locusts on the six-car yellow-and-green streamliner. I was afraid I wouldn't get a seat for my 339-mile ride, but I had underestimated one of the virtues of the bilevel concept: high capacity. Each bilevel coach could seat 96 passengers, nearly twice as many as a single-level car.

I commandeered a comfortable, cushiony individual reclining seat in an upper-level area of the second-to-last coach. Nonetheless, the train was filled nearly to capacity. Lesson No. 1: the *Flambeau* was an integral component of the busy, heavily populated, 200-plus-mile Chicago–Milwaukee–Green Bay corridor, served by six Chicago & North Western trains in each direction and on two different lines north of Milwaukee. (Milwaukee Road also served this corridor, but with only one train each way north of Milwaukee.)

We departed Chicago on time at 11:20 A.M. behind two back-to-back Electro-Motive diesels. Our train comprised a baggage-mail-tavern car, one coach, diner, and three more coaches. The *Flambeau*

Some students of streamliners feel that passenger-train design reached its zenith with the introduction of the 1947 *Twin Cities Zephyr*, foretold by the 1945 unveiling of the first dome car (built by Burlington) and the 1946 debut of the General Motors/Pullman-Standard all-dome *Train of Tomorrow*. The *Morning (Twin) Zephyr* has just pulled out of Chicago Union Station in April 1963 with a combination of cars that includes extra non-*Zephyr* cars at the head end (possibly for holiday travel or a group movement), and the first dome on the train is one of Burlington's two homemade domes. *Alvin Schultze*

wasted little time covering the 84 miles to Milwaukee—stops at Evanston, Waukegan, Kenosha, and Racine notwithstanding.

Near downtown Milwaukee shortly before 1:00 P.M., the *Flambeau* entered Milwaukee Road rails to reach the new passenger depot where in 1965 Milwaukee Road and C&NW operations had been consolidated. After departing Milwaukee, the train negotiated some rough Milwaukee Road track on the run to Canco Junction on the north side of the city. Bracing myself against anything bolted to the floor, I made my way forward for lunch.

The new Wabash streamliner *Blue Bird* poses for its official portrait near Forest Park near downtown St. Louis, Missouri, in 1950. Clad in blue and stainless steel with yellow-gold trim, the *Blue Bird* was one of the most beautiful trains built by the Budd Company. Unfortunately, the trainset did not remain in its as-delivered arrangement for very long, with Wabash reassigning two of the dome coaches to other trains. Even the dome parlor-observation car was reassigned to the *Banner Blue*, the *Blue Bird*'s sister train on the Chicago–St. Louis route. *Wabash Railroad*

The bright, cheery diner was a 1941 veteran of the Chicago-Minneapolis *Twin Cities "400,"* rebuilt in 1958 for bilevel *"400"* service. I was seated across the table from a woman who had just been served a club sandwich luncheon, but it seems the train's lurching "voyage" up the Milwaukee Road to Canco had tempered her appetite, and she graciously pushed the plate across the table to me. "Here, I think you'll enjoy this more than I will." I did.

At Canco the *Flambeau* returned to home rails, and the ride smoothed out somewhat. Northbound, the *Flambeau* operated on C&NW's Shore Route, and the trip up to Green Bay gave several nice views of Lake Michigan. Arrival at Green Bay at 3:35 P.M. ushered in a complete transformation of the train as most passengers detrained. Simultaneous with our arrival in the depot was that of the southbound *Flambeau "400."* We had a scheduled 25-minute stop here, so I got off the train to watch lesson No. 2: efficient equipment utilization. Our locomotives pulled the baggage-mail-tavern car, first coach, and diner from the remaining three coaches of the northbound train and transferred them directly to the rear of the southbound *Flambeau*, which had arrived from Ashland with a single locomotive and three coaches. So that set of cars did double duty, serving both *Flambeaus* in a single day. Additionally, one of the locomotives from my train was transferred to the southbound. By 4 P.M. both trains were "buttoned up" and ready to resume their journeys.

The *Flambeau* had also undergone a change in personality. What had been a crowded, high-speed corridor train from Chicago to Green Bay became a half-empty, leisurely local run. We departed Green Bay and began poking into the piney lake lands of northern Wisconsin. Whereas the *Flambeau* had been blazing along at 80 miles per hour before Green Bay, the train now held a more relaxed gait of perhaps 55—and even less as it branched onto other secondary lines at Eland and Monico. Stops now were frequent and at stations (some without depots) with northwoodsy and Indian names—Shawano,

Summit Lake, Pelican Lake—where a passenger or two would hop off and head to resort homes nestled against cool lakes painted gold by the evening sun.

At 7:15 P.M. we rolled into Rhinelander, the center of commerce and tourism for northern Wisconsin. My family members were among the large crowd at the depot greeting arriving friends and relatives. The connecting bus to Eagle River and Land O' Lakes (of butter fame) stood nearby ready to load transferees. Clearly, the *Flambeau "400'''*s arrival was an event. My trip was done, but the *Flambeau* still had another 114 miles to trek through Lake Tomahawk, Lac du Flambeau, and then Ironwood, Michigan, and other locales before terminating at Ashland at 10:45 P.M., 11 hours, 25 minutes and 452.7 miles after leaving Chicago.

Domeliner Cousins

The apex of the regional streamliner might be best represented by two different trains: Chicago, Burlington & Quincy's 1947 *Twin Zephyrs* and Wabash's 1950 *Blue Bird*. The postwar edition of the *Twin Zephyrs*—racers of the 437-mile Chicago-Minneapolis run—introduced the revolutionary Vista-Dome car to U.S. railroading. The Budd Company built two eight-car stainless-steel train sets, each with a baggage-tavern car, four Vista-Dome coaches, diner, parlor car, and Vista-Dome parlor observation car. The 1947 *Twin Zephyrs* were stellar examples of how transportation technology could be perfectly united with eye-catching aesthetics and design—an accomplishment that has since been lost on U.S. passenger railroading.

I spent many hours aboard the *Twin Zephyrs*, their high-speed, double-daily schedules providing convenient travel options to northern Illinoisans. I saw them at their best (with all-matching cars), rode them during some quirky moments (detouring through my hometown of Rockford because of mainline blockage), and witnessed them in unbecoming situations (wrecked at Lee, Illinois). I rode the final eastbound *Afternoon Zephyr* on May 1, 1971, and now 28

Dining-car waiters stand at the ready on Norfolk & Western's *Blue Bird* in 1966. The diner's interior decor remained virtually unchanged 16 years after it was built by Budd.

years later live at "*Zephyr* Acres" adjacent to the line on which the *Twins* raced for 36 years.

I held nearly equally high esteem for the *Blue Bird*, the preeminent streamliner of Wabash Railroad's 286-mile Chicago–St. Louis main line. No surprise here; the Budd-built *Blue Bird* was nearly identical to the 1947 Twin *Zephyr* train sets, with a baggage-lunch-counter-lounge car, three Vista-Dome coaches, diner-lounge, and Vista-Dome parlor-observation car. A Pullman-Standard dome parlor-

lounge was added in 1952 because of the demand for parlor accommodations.

Wabash rebuffed Budd's insistence that its stainless-steel cars should not be painted when the railroad specified a tasteful application of blue paint to some segments of the car bodies, leaving others *au naturale*: Gold lettering and pin-striping were the perfect final touch. The result was a domeliner of stunning beauty pulled by an Electro-Motive E7 diesel painted in the Wabash's intricate blue-gray-and-white livery. It became known by locals as the "bubble train" because of its domed profile.

The interior decor—carpeting, drapes, Venetian blinds, tabletops—played on the blue theme, incorporating blues and grays accented by black and rust. Car bulkheads featured murals painted in oil by artist Auriel Bessemer. Can you imagine original oil paintings today as part of a train decor? Such was the idyllic 1950s.

Three of us friends rode the *Blue Bird* in 1967 during a trip from Chicago to Kansas City by way of St. Louis. By this time, the *Blue Bird* was an interesting mix of cars, quite different from the original train. Early on, Wabash began shuffling its passenger-car fleet, and matching train sets became a thing of the past. For example, Wabash reassigned two *Blue Bird* Vista-Dome coaches to the Chicago–St. Louis *Banner Blue* and Kansas City–St. Louis *City of Kansas City*, elevating those trains to "Domeliner" status. After Wabash and Nickel Plate were merged into the Norfolk & Western in 1964, the car pool included equipment from Nickel Plate's defunct Chicago-Buffalo streamliners as well. Thus on our late afternoon ride out of Dearborn Station, we had only two true *Blue Bird* cars in our train: the original Budd diner-lounge and the P-S dome parlor-lounge. Everything else was former Nickel Plate.

We splurged for first-class seating in the dome parlor-lounge, which made us lowly college students feel like rail barons. Why? We were the only passengers to purchase parlor seating on that day's run, and we had the whole car to ourselves.

Two traits of the Wabash of yore—hospitality and good food—were still evident on our train. As twilight set in across the pancake-flat agricultural countryside of northeast Illinois, we headed for dinner. Upon entering the mostly empty diner-lounge, I raised my camera to record the car's interior, prompting the steward to rush toward me shaking his finger.

"Please, sir, let my men present themselves properly!" the steward spoke out. And with that, the waiters snapped to attention while I snapped the photo! The steward smiled, thanked me, and seated us. And like good college students, we chowed down on hamburgers, which on the Wabash had always come highly recommended. We washed it all down with iced tea made the *only* way iced tea should be made: freshly brewed and steaming, poured over chunks of clear ice in tall glasses (with a bowl of extra ice on the side). As we finished up with another Wabash specialty, homemade apple pie, I imagined what it might have been like dining on this car in 1950 shortly after the *Blue Bird*'s inaugural, with men in broad-lapel suits and women wearing salad-plate hats seated at the tables that now lay empty around us.

Later, from the dome, we watched St. Louis' Gateway Arch come into view as we crossed the Mississippi River on Merchants Bridge. At 10:25 P.M., the *Blue Bird* backed into Union Station. Now we went from the sublime to the ridiculous: Our connecting train to Kansas City, Missouri Pacific train 19, had 28 cars—27 mail and express and one coach brimming with passengers trying to sleep while sitting up. We were college students again.

INDEX